Gospel Light's

BIG BOOK OF TIME FILLERS

GRA

Bible-based activities to enrich kids' learning

Make good use of unscheduled time

Discussion games, riddles, activity ideas and more!

CD-ROM INCLUDED

Reproducible!

Linda Massey Weddle

GUIDELINES FOR PHOTOCOPYING PAGES

Editorial Staff

Founder, Dr. Henrietta Mears • **Publisher,** William T. Greig • **Senior Consulting Publisher,** Dr. Elmer L. Towns • **Senior Managing Editor,** Sheryl Haystead • **Senior Consulting Editor,** Wesley Haystead, M.S.Ed. • **Senior Editor, Biblical and Theological Issues,** Bayard Taylor, M.Div. • **Contributing Editors,** Debbie Barber, Janis Halverson, Lisa Key • **Art Director,** Lenndy Pollard • **Designer,** Annette M. Chavez

How to Use This Book

If you are the children's pastor,

1. Read "Introduction" on pages 5-6 and briefly skim through several sections to get an overview of *The Big Book of Time Fillers*.
2. Collect and store in each classroom or in a central location the supplies suggested on page 6.
3. Make copies of this book and provide to teachers. Tip: Rather than distributing all the sections at once, provide a different section every month or so. You may also choose to select and distribute sections that you think would be most usable for a particular class or program.

If you are a teacher or small-group leader,

1. Read "Introduction" on pages 5-6 and briefly skim through several sections to get an overview of *The Big Book of Time Fillers*.
2. If the supplies listed on page 6 are not readily available to you, collect and store in a convenient location.
3. Use activities as needed to enrich or extend your teaching.

Contents

Activities

Introduction

We love children's ministry, but there are those moments in all our lives, when things don't go exactly the way we planned—

- The teacher assigned to the lesson calls on her cell phone to tell you she has a flat tire.
- ALL your regular teachers come down with the flu—on the same night.
- Your well-planned 20-minute lesson only takes 10.
- The DVD is a perfect discussion starter, but the DVD player isn't working (or was snagged by the youth pastor).
- The pastor, special speaker or guest musicians are going WAY over time.
- Your well-prepared plan isn't working and the kids are growing more restless by the minute.

We've all been there. We've all had those moments when we wish we had an instantaneous emergency plan.

That's what this book is all about. Ideas, quizzes, riddles, mini-teaching plans and more to bring value to those otherwise empty (and probably chaotic) minutes.

So, look through the book and choose some ideas to have ready for the next time this happens to you.

Be Ready

Work with at least one other teacher, so when those moments happen, you can keep talking to the class, while the other teacher automatically gathers whatever you need for one of the activities. While waiting for the teacher to get ready, share a fun fact or riddle, play a game or tell a story. You don't want nothing-going-on time. Teachers panic. Children take advantage of the inactivity and start talking, running around the room, poking each other and whatever else they can think of to do.

We suggest you copy (and laminate, if you'd like) the pages provided for use in Letters in the Lines (see p. 140), Sketching a Scene (see p. 143) and Bible Story Charades (see p. 148). Cut apart the pages and store in individual containters. Children get excited about these games and excited about having a turn. Sometimes, however, when they're actually chosen, they freeze. They can't think of a word or Bible event to use. Meanwhile, other children are wildly waving their arms around to have a turn and things quickly can get out of hand. Or, the child who is chosen uses a word (for Letters in the Lines) that he doesn't know how to spell. That means a whispered conversation with a teacher between every guess ("Is the letter in the word? Where do I put it?"). Having the children choose the word or event from the container keeps the game moving and provides the correct spelling.

Collect the supplies, make copies of the quizzes . . . and you'll be ready to go at a moment's notice!

Basic Supplies to Have on Hand

1. Bibles, Bible dictionary and Bible concordance.
2. Paper—all kinds, including construction paper, white copy paper, plain postcards, newsprint and butcher paper. (You can now purchase Post-it sketch pads and banner paper which are perfect for displaying some of the artwork the children make.)
3. Pencils, pens, crayons and markers. Make sure the markers actually work! Fresh ones will produce bright colors.
4. Glue, masking tape, scissors, stapler and hole punch.
5. Whiteboard and/or chalkboard. If possible, have a couple of these (or more) on hand for when you divide your class into teams.
6. One or more digital cameras. Many companies make digital cameras which are designed for children to use. Because you can use cameras in many activities, they are a good addition to your classroom. (Kids can take as many pictures as they want and save them to a computer. The cost will come in the printing.)
7. Game supplies (soft or foam balls, tennis balls, beanbags, large containers, paper cups, coins for each child).
8. Prizes. Keep your eyes open for small prizes (inexpensive party favors or bite-size wrapped pieces of candy) you can keep on hand to reward winning individuals or teams. Keep the prizes in a prize box and store in a convenient place.
9. Church information (names of staff members and shut-ins, church events, etc.) and missions resources (globe or world map, prayer cards or other information about the missionaries your church or denomination supports, children's missionary biographies, a CD of children's music from another country).
10. Clear Con-Tact paper or access to a laminator.
11. Children's music CD and player.

Supplies for Specific Activities

1. Samples of ads from magazines (see p. 32).
2. Plastic page protectors and three-ring binders (see p. 82).
3. Play dough (see p. 94).
4. Wooden blocks (see p. 99).
5. Stopwatch (or watch with second hand) (see p. 119).
6. Knife-sharpener and knife from home or church kitchen (see p. 128).
7. Plastic containers to store word cards (see pp. 141, 143, 149).
8. Props such as classroom objects, preschool toys, etc. (see p. 146).
9. Child-safe cleaning supplies (see p. 159).
10. Various colors of cellophane (see p. 164).
11. Fabric and felt (see p. 170).
12. Real or pretend microphone (see p. 175).

Leading a Child to Christ

Many adult Christians look back to their childhood years as the time when they accepted Christ as Savior. As children mature, they will grow in their understanding of the difference between right and wrong. They will also develop a sense of their own need for forgiveness and feel a growing desire to have a personal relationship with God.

However, the younger the child is the more limited he or she will be in understanding abstract terms. Children of all ages are likely to be inconsistent in following through on their intentions and commitments. Therefore, they need thoughtful, patient guidance in coming to know Christ personally and continuing to grow in Him.

Pray

Ask God to prepare the students in your group to receive the good news about Jesus and prepare you to communicate effectively with them.

Present the Good News

Use words and phrases that students understand. Avoid symbolism that will confuse these literal-minded thinkers. Remember that each child's learning will be at different places on the spectrum of understanding. Discuss these points slowly enough to allow time for thinking and comprehending.

   a. God wants you to become His child. Do you know why God wants you in His family? (See 1 John 3:1.)
   b. You and I and all the people in the world have done wrong things. The Bible word for doing wrong is "sin." What do you think should happen to us when we sin? (See Romans 6:23.)
   c. God loves you so much, He sent His Son to die on the cross for your sins. Because Jesus never sinned, He is the only One who can take the punishment for your sins. On the third day after Jesus died, God brought Him back to life. (See 1 Corinthians 15:3-4; 1 John 4:14.)
   d. Are you sorry for your sins? Tell God that you are. Do you believe Jesus died to take the punishment for your sins and that He rose again? Tell God that, too. If you tell God you are sorry for your sins and tell Him you do believe and accept Jesus' death to take away your sins—God forgives all your sin. (See 1 John 1:9.)
   e. The Bible says that when you believe that Jesus is God's Son and that He is alive today, you receive God's gift of eternal life. This gift makes you a child of God. This means God is with you now and forever. (See John 1:12; 3:16.)

Give students many opportunities to think about what it means to be a Christian; expose them to a variety of lessons and descriptions of the meaning of salvation to aid their understanding.

Talk Personally with the Student

Talking about salvation one-on-one creates the opportunity to ask and answer questions. Ask questions that move the student beyond simple yes or no answers or recitation of memorized information. Ask open-ended, what-do-you-think questions such as:

   • "Why do you think it's important to . . . ?"
   • "What are some things you really like about Jesus?"
   • "Why do you think that Jesus had to die because of wrong things you and I have done?"
   • "What difference do you think it makes for a person to be forgiven?"

When students use abstract terms or phrases they have learned previously, such as "accepting Christ into my heart," ask them to tell you what the term or phrase means in different words. Answers to these open-ended questions will help you discern how much the student does or does not understand.

Offer Opportunities Without Pressure

Children normally desire to please adults. This characteristic makes them vulnerable to being unintentionally manipulated by well-meaning adults. A good way to guard against coercing a student's response is to simply pause periodically and ask, "Would you like to hear more about this now or at another time?" Loving acceptance of the student, even when he or she is not fully interested in pursuing the matter, is crucial in building and maintaining positive attitudes toward becoming part of God's family.

Give Time to Think and Pray

There is great value in encouraging a student to think and pray about what you have said before making a response. Also allow moments for quiet thinking about questions you have asked.

Respect the Student's Response

Whether or not a student declares faith in Jesus Christ, there is a need for adults to accept the student's action. There is also a need to realize that a student's initial responses to Jesus are just the beginning of a lifelong process of growing in the faith.

Guide the Student in Further Growth

There are several important parts in the nurturing process.

a. Talk regularly about your relationship with God. As you talk about your relationship, the student will begin to feel that it's OK to talk about such things. Then you can comfortably ask the student to share his or her thoughts and feelings, and you can encourage the student to ask questions of you.

b. Prepare the student to deal with doubts. Emphasize that certainty about salvation is not dependent on our feelings or doing enough good deeds. Show the student places in God's Word that clearly declare that salvation comes by grace through faith. (See John 1:12; Ephesians 2:8-9; Hebrews 11:6; 1 John 5:11.)

c. Teach the student to confess all sins. This means agreeing with God that we really have sinned. Assure the student that confession always results in forgiveness. (See 1 John 1:9.)

The Preschool Child and Salvation

- The young child is easily attracted to Jesus. Jesus is a warm, sympathetic person who obviously likes children, and children readily like Him. These early perceptions prepare the foundation for the child to receive Christ as Savior and to desire to follow His example in godly living. While some preschoolers may indeed pray to become a member of God's family, accepting Jesus as their Savior, expect wide variation in children's readiness for this important step. Allow the Holy Spirit room to work within His own timetable.

- Talk simply. Phrases such as "born again" or "Jesus in my heart" are symbolic and far beyond a young child's understanding. Focus on how God makes people a part of His family.

- Present the love of Jesus by both your actions and your words in order to lay a foundation for a child to receive Christ as Savior. Look for opportunities in every lesson to talk with a young child who wants to know more about Jesus.

Answering the Questions

Goal: To provide a fun, active way for children to answer and discuss questions about Bible truths.

What Do I Need?

- Bible
- One of the discussion activities from pages 10-14
- A copy of one set of Discussion Cards (see pp. 15-31)
- Scissors
- Materials as listed for the activity

How Do I Do It?

- The activities in this section require few, if any, materials, are easy to set up and are a fun way to review the Bible truth of any lesson.
- Cut apart one set of Discussion Cards (see pp. 15-31).
- Lead children in the discussion activity you chose.

Take It Another Step

Invite children to make up their own questions after hearing a Bible story or reading a Bible passage.

Behind-the-Back Toss

What Do I Need?

- Soft ball or beanbag

How Do I Do It?

- Children stand in a group. A volunteer stands in front of the group with back facing the group. Children in group mix themselves up. Volunteer tosses soft ball or beanbag over shoulder. Child in group who catches the ball or beanbag answers a question from the Discussion Cards. Repeat with other volunteers.

Ball Toss

What Do I Need?

- Large container (wastepaper basket, bucket, etc.)
- Soft ball or beanbag

How Do I Do It?

- Place large container in the center of the room.
- Children stand about 4 feet (1.2 m) from container. Children take turns tossing ball or beanbag into the container. When a ball or beanbag lands in the container, child answers a question from the Discussion Cards. Continue as time permits.

Chair Trade

What Do I Need?

- Chairs

How Do I Do It?

- Arrange chairs in circle. Children sit in chairs.
- Close your eyes. While you count slowly to three, children randomly trade chairs. Keeping your eyes closed, call out the name of one of your children. The child sitting to the right of the child whose name you called answers a question from the Discussion Cards. Repeat, calling other children's names.

Circle Spin

What Do I Need?

- No supplies needed for this activity

How Do I Do It?

- Children stand in a circle. Volunteer stands in the middle of the circle with eyes closed. Volunteer spins around several times, stops and points. Whichever child the volunteer is pointing at answers a question from the Discussion Cards.

Coin Cups

What Do I Need?

- Paper cups
- Coins

How Do I Do It?

- Divide class into pairs. Give each child a cup and a coin. Ask a question. Children place coins in cups. Call "Heads" or "Tails." Children turn cups over so that coins fall out onto table or floor. Each child whose coin shows the side called tells his or her partner how he or she would answer the question from the Discussion Cards. If both children's coins are showing the named side, both children tell answers. If neither children's coins are showing the named side, children place coins into cups and play again. Invite several volunteers to tell answers to the whole class. Repeat with other questions.

Discussion Dots

What Do I Need?

- Marker
- Large sheet of paper

How Do I Do It?

- Draw a row of 15 dots across a large sheet of paper.
- Children take turns crossing off either one or two dots. (It is not necessary for the dots to be next to each other.) Child who crosses off the last dot answers a question from the Discussion Cards. Repeat the activity with another row of dots, answering questions as time permits.

Answering the Questions
Draw Straws

What Do I Need?

- Straws or paper strips
- Scissors

How Do I Do It?

- Cut straws or paper strips into equal lengths, one for each child. Cut one again so that it is shorter than the others.
- Hold straws or papers in your hand so that they look even. Each child takes a straw or paper. Child with the shorter straw or paper answers a question from the Discussion Cards.

Group and Regroup

What Do I Need?

- No supplies needed for this activity

How Do I Do It?

- Children walk around the room. Call out a number (from two to five). Group divides into groups of the number called. For example, if the number two is called, children stand in groups of two. Any child left without a group answers a question from the Discussion Cards. Repeat as time permits.

Handy Pileup

What Do I Need?

- No supplies needed for this activity

How Do I Do It?

- Form groups of three or four children. One child puts a hand palm-down on table or floor. The other children add their own hands one at a time to the pile. The hand on the bottom is withdrawn and added to the top of the pile. Continue until you signal stop. Child whose hand is on the bottom of the pile answers a question from the Discussion Cards. Repeat as time permits.

12

Answering the Questions
Number Guess

What Do I Need?

- No supplies needed for this activity

How Do I Do It?

- Secretly choose a number from zero to five. Children stand with hands behind their backs. At your signal, children guess number by showing number of fingers. Each child whose guess matches that of the teacher answers a question from the Discussion Cards.

Odd or Even

What Do I Need?

- No supplies needed for this activity

How Do I Do It?

- Divide class into pairs. One child chooses "odd" and the other chooses "even." Each child puts a hand behind his or her back and together they count "One, two, three." On "three," both children thrust a hand in front of them with one to five fingers showing.
If the total number of fingers is odd, the player who chose "odd" answers a question. If the total is even, the other player answers a question from the Discussion Cards.

Over/Under

What Do I Need?

- Small object to pass around (marker, eraser, etc.)
- Children's music CD and player

How Do I Do It?

- Children stand in a line. As you play music, the first child passes object over his or her head, the second child passes it between his or her legs, and so on to the end of the line. Last child in line brings object to the front of the line and continues passing object. When the music stops, child holding the object answers a question from the Discussion Cards. Continue as time permits.

Answering the Questions
Telephone

What Do I Need?

- No supplies needed for this activity

How Do I Do It?

- Divide class into groups of no more than six to eight. Each group forms a circle. Whisper a question from the Discussion Cards to one child in each circle. Child passes the question to the next person by whispering it to him or her. The last person to receive the question in each circle says it aloud (clarify as needed). Volunteers answer the question. Repeat with other questions as time permits, each time beginning with a different child in the circle.

The Most

What Do I Need?

- No supplies needed for this activity

How Do I Do It?

- Children stand in groups of three or four. Ask a question. In each group, child with the most letters in his or her last name answers a question from the Discussion Cards. Repeat as time permits, asking new questions, changing groups and using other categories such as fewest letters in name, nearest birthday, wearing the most green, etc.

Thumbs Up/Thumbs Down

What Do I Need?

- No supplies needed for this activity

How Do I Do It?

- Count "One, two, three." On "three" all children make a thumbs-up or a thumbs-down motion with both hands. Without looking at children, call "Thumbs-up" or "Thumbs-down." Volunteer from child holding thumbs in position called answers a question from the Discussion Cards.

Answering the Questions
Discussion Cards - Psalm 23

What do you know about how a shepherd cares for sheep? What do you learn about God from Psalm 23?

Psalm 23

What tough times does Psalm 23 talk about? How did the writer say God helped him in those tough times?

Psalm 23

In what ways does the writer of Psalm 23 describe God's help and comfort in verses 1-4? When have you experienced God's help and comfort in these ways?

Psalm 23

When you think about the hard situations described in Psalm 23, which descriptions of God's help are most appealing to you? Why?

Psalm 23

The writer of Psalm 23 describes a green pasture and quiet waters. What scene would you choose to describe times when God has comforted you?

Psalm 23

In Psalm 23:4-6, what do you think is the writer's attitude about the future?

Psalm 23

15

Answering the Questions
Discussion Cards - Psalm 51:1-4,10-12

What words does the writer of Psalm 51:1 use to describe God? What ideas about God do you get from those words?

Psalm 51:1-4,10-12

In Psalm 51:10, what do you think might be different between the two requests ("a pure heart" and "a steadfast spirit")? What might be the same about them?

Psalm 51:1-4,10-12

What does the writer of Psalm 51 ask God to do in verses 1-4? Why? When are some times kids your age might want to say words like these to God?

Psalm 51:1-4,10-12

In Psalm 51:1-4, what words refer to wrong things a person has done? If you were explaining these verses to a younger child, what words might you use instead?

Psalm 51:1-4,10-12

How does the writer of Psalm 51 ask God to help him in verses 10-12? Choose one request and tell why a person who sins needs that from God.

Psalm 51:1-4,10-12

How would you say Psalm 51:10, 11 or 12 in simpler words?

Psalm 51:1-4,10-12

Answering the Questions

Discussion Cards - Psalm 139:1-3,13-16

In Psalm 139:1-3, what words are used that mean the same as "know"? What are some specific things God knows about us?

Psalm 139:1-3,13-16

If Psalm 139:1-3,13-16 was everything you knew about God, how would you describe Him?

Psalm 139:1-3,13-16

You have been asked to design a bumper sticker that states a main idea from Psalm 139:1-3. What would your bumper sticker say?

Psalm 139:1-3,13-16

When you read about how well God knows us in Psalm 139:1-3,13-16, how do you feel?

Psalm 139:1-3,13-16

What are some reasons Psalm 139:13-16 might help kids your age trust God?

Psalm 139:1-3,13-16

According to Psalm 139:14, what should be our response when we think about how God has made us?

Psalm 139:1-3,13-16

Answering the Questions
Discussion Cards - Psalm 146:7-10

In Psalm 146:7-10, what different actions of God are described? What do you learn about God from these actions?

Psalm 146:7-10

How might the words in Psalm 146:7-10 be comforting to someone who is discouraged by big problems?

Psalm 146:7-10

What ways to treat other people are described in Psalm 146:7-10? What words would you use to describe someone who treated people in these ways?

Psalm 146:7-10

What kinds of situations are described in these verses? Why might a person facing one of the situations in Psalm 146:7-10 want to praise God?

Psalm 146:7-10

Psalm 146:7-10 describes some ways that God helps people in difficult situations. When have you known or heard of someone in a difficult situation? What could a kid your age do to help a person in that situation?

Psalm 146:7-10

What are some ways kids your age could show compassion to people like those described in Psalm 146:7-10?

Psalm 146:7-10

Discussion Cards - Proverbs 3:3-6

Proverbs 3:3 says that we should keep love and faithfulness close to us. What do you think is the difference between love and faithfulness? Why do you think they should be so important to us?

Proverbs 3:3-6

Proverbs 3:3,4 says that showing love and faithfulness will give us a good name, or reputation. Why do you think it is important to have a good name, or reputation, in God's sight? Who are some people you have heard of who have good reputations?

Proverbs 3:3-6

Proverbs 3:3-6 tells us to show love and faithfulness constantly. What can we do to remember to show God's love and faithfulness to others?

Proverbs 3:3-6

Following Proverbs 3:3,4, what can people do to develop good names, or reputations, for themselves?

Proverbs 3:3-6

What are some things you can do to obey Proverbs 3:3 by showing love or faithfulness to a friend? To a family member?

Proverbs 3:3-6

Proverbs 3:5,6 tells us that when we trust in God's Word, He will make our paths straight. What are some other ways to describe what happens if we trust in God's Word?

Proverbs 3:3-6

Answering the Questions
Discussion Cards - Matthew 5:3-9

Seven times in Matthew 5:3-9 Jesus uses the word "blessed." What does it mean for someone to be blessed? What are some other words that communicate a similar idea?

Matthew 5:3-9

Read Matther 5:6. What might a person who hungers and thirsts after righteousness, or goodness, do?

Matthew 5:3-9

According to Matthew 5:5, Jesus says that meek, or humble, people will inherit the earth. What do you think that means?

Matthew 5:3-9

In Matthew 5:7, Jesus talked about showing mercy. What's so great about being shown mercy? How can you show mercy to others?

Matthew 5:3-9

Read Mathew 5:5. Who do you know that is humble? Why do you think this person is humble? How can kids your age show meekness?

Matthew 5:3-9

Read Matthew 5:8. How many different ways can you think of to say that someone is sincere, or pure in heart?

Matthew 5:3-9

20

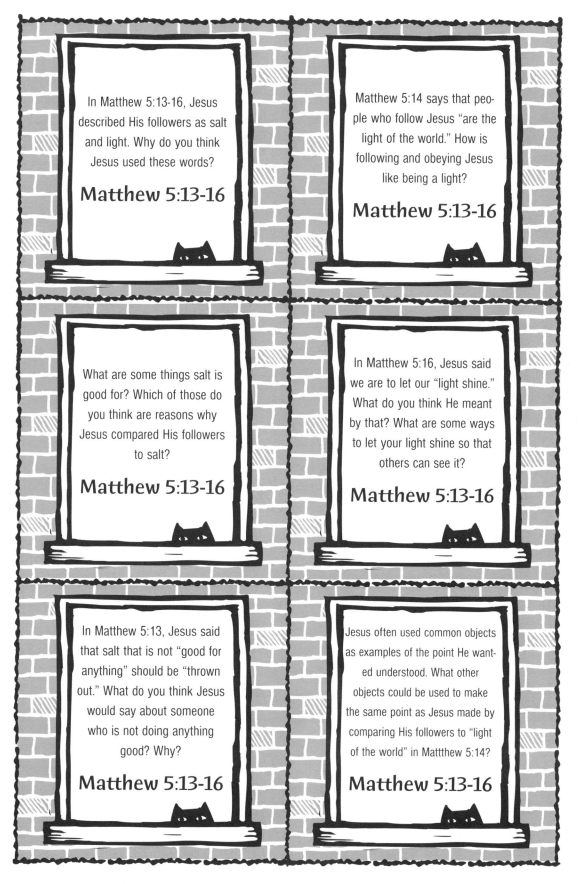

In Matthew 5:13-16, Jesus described His followers as salt and light. Why do you think Jesus used these words?

Matthew 5:13-16

Matthew 5:14 says that people who follow Jesus "are the light of the world." How is following and obeying Jesus like being a light?

Matthew 5:13-16

What are some things salt is good for? Which of those do you think are reasons why Jesus compared His followers to salt?

Matthew 5:13-16

In Matthew 5:16, Jesus said we are to let our "light shine." What do you think He meant by that? What are some ways to let your light shine so that others can see it?

Matthew 5:13-16

In Matthew 5:13, Jesus said that salt that is not "good for anything" should be "thrown out." What do you think Jesus would say about someone who is not doing anything good? Why?

Matthew 5:13-16

Jesus often used common objects as examples of the point He wanted understood. What other objects could be used to make the same point as Jesus made by comparing His followers to "light of the world" in Mattthew 5:14?

Matthew 5:13-16

Discussion Cards - Matthew 6:9-13

In Matthew 6:9-13, Jesus taught His disciples how to pray. What have you learned from other people about how to pray?

Matthew 6:9-13

In Matthew 6:9, Jesus said to pray that the name of God will be "hallowed," or treated with great respect and honor. What are some ways people treat God's name disrespectfully? Respectfully?

Matthew 6:9-13

In Matthew 6:9-13, what are some things Jesus said we should pray about? When might be a good time to pray "hallowed be your name" or one of the other phrases in the verses?

Matthew 6:9-13

In Matthew 6:10, Jesus prayed for something so important that He asked for it twice, saying the same thing in two ways. What do you think He wants to happen when He says that, "your kingdom come, your will be done"?

Matthew 6:9-13

In Matthew 6:9, what name did Jesus call God? How is God like a father?

Matthew 6:9-13

In Matthew 6:11, why do you think Jesus said to pray, "Give us today our daily bread"? Besides food, what are some things we need every day that might be included in this request?

Matthew 6:9-13

Answering the Questions
Discussion Cards - Matthew 6:19-21, 24

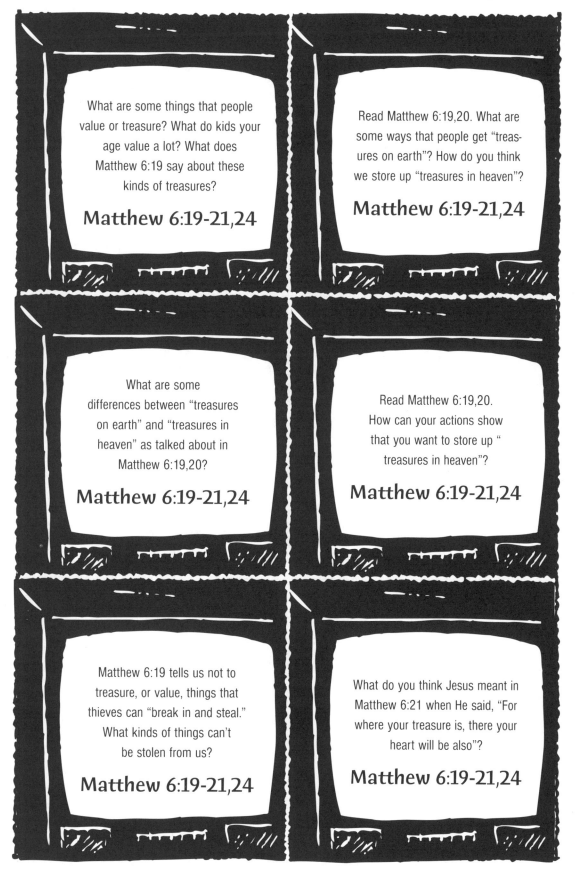

What are some things that people value or treasure? What do kids your age value a lot? What does Matthew 6:19 say about these kinds of treasures?

Matthew 6:19-21,24

Read Matthew 6:19,20. What are some ways that people get "treasures on earth"? How do you think we store up "treasures in heaven"?

Matthew 6:19-21,24

What are some differences between "treasures on earth" and "treasures in heaven" as talked about in Matthew 6:19,20?

Matthew 6:19-21,24

Read Matthew 6:19,20. How can your actions show that you want to store up " treasures in heaven"?

Matthew 6:19-21,24

Matthew 6:19 tells us not to treasure, or value, things that thieves can "break in and steal." What kinds of things can't be stolen from us?

Matthew 6:19-21,24

What do you think Jesus meant in Matthew 6:21 when He said, "For where your treasure is, there your heart will be also"?

Matthew 6:19-21,24

Answering the Questions

Discussion Cards - Romans 8:35,37-39

When might kids your age feel that God doesn't love them? Why? What does Romans 8:35,37 say that could help someone who doesn't feel loved by God?

Romans 8:35, 37-39

Romans 8:38,39 lists things that cannot separate us from God's love or cause God to stop loving us. What specific situations could you add to that list?

Romans 8:35, 37-39

Paul faced all the troubles listed in Romans 8:35. Which of these troubles sounds most difficult to you? How do you think God might help someone in one of these situations?

Romans 8:35, 37-39

What are some things in the present that might worry kids your age? In the future? What does Romans 8:38,39 promise us?

Romans 8:35, 37-39

What does Romans 8:37 say we are when we face big problems? How are we able to conquer such terrible problems?

Romans 8:35, 37-39

Choose one of the situations in Romans 8:35. How can God help someone who is in this situation?

Romans 8:35, 37-39

Answering the Questions
Discussion Cards - Romans 12:9-14,17-21

Imagine that our class was being graded on how well we obey Romans 12:9,10. What grade do you think we would get? What are some actions that might raise our grade? Lower our grade?

Romans 12:9-14,17-21

How can your words show that you care about others' needs and interests? How can your words demonstrate hospitality or generosity? How can your actions show these things?

Romans 12:9-14,17-21

Which of the instructions in Romans 12:9-14 do you think would help kids your age the most in showing God's love to other kids at school? Why?

Romans 12:9-14,17-21

When are some times kids your age feel persecuted or mistreated? How can kids your age obey Romans 12:14 and do good to the people who mistreat them in situations like these?

Romans 12:9-14,17-21

What is one way you could obey the instructions in Romans 12:10 when you have a disagreement with a friend?

Romans 12:9-14,17-21

What difference would it make in your school or your neighborhood if kids followed the instructions in Romans 12:17?

Romans 12:9-14,17-21

25

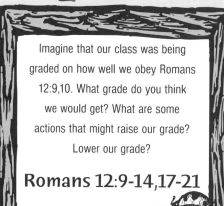
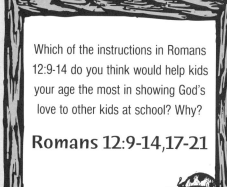
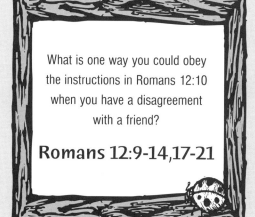

Discussion Cards - 1 Corinthians 13:4-8a

Which actions described in
1 Corinthians 13:4-8a could you
do to help the people you live with?
What might happen as a result
of your actions?

1 Corinthians 13:4-8a

According to 1 Corinthians 13:5,
what is the love God wants us
to have not like? When is it
hard not to have these attitudes?

1 Corinthians 13:4-8a

How did Jesus demonstrate the
kind of love described in
1 Corinthians 13:4-8a?

1 Corinthians 13:4-8a

1 Corinthians 13:6 says love "rejoices
with the truth." How is being truthful
a way to show love? How does not
rejoicing in evil show the way God
wants us to love?

1 Corinthians 13:4-8a

How could you show the kind
of love described in
1 Corinthians 13:4 to a friend?
To someone who is not a friend?

1 Corinthians 13:4-8a

1 Corinthians 13:7 lists four ways God
wants us to love others. What is a way
a kid your age can show love to a
friend in these ways?

1 Corinthians 13:4-8a

Answering the Questions
Discussion Cards - Galatians 5:22,23

Galatians 5:22,23 lists nine character traits, or ways of acting, that God's Spirit helps us develop. When have you seen someone show one of these character traits?

Galatians 5:22,23

What can a person do to develop the characteristics listed in Galatians 5:22,23?

Galatians 5:22,23

Read Galatians 5:22. What might remind you to show love? Joy? Peace?

Galatians 5:22,23

What do you think the last part of Galatians 5:23 means? Why would there be no law against showing the fruit of the Spirit?

Galatians 5:22,23

Think of a time you have seen someone demonstrate some of the characteristics listed in Galatians 5:22,23. What happened because the person acted in that way?

Galatians 5:22,23

What does fruit need to grow? Why do you think the character traits in Galatians 5:22,23 are referred to as fruit? What can help you grow this spiritual fruit?

Galatians 5:22,23

Discussion Cards - Ephesians 4:1-6

Paul, one of Jesus' followers, wrote Ephesians 4:1-6 to describe God's plan for the people who believe in Him. What do you think is the most important instruction that Paul wrote in Ephesians 4:1-3 for the church family?

Ephesians 4:1-6

How many different ways can you think of to say what Ephesians 4:3 tells us to make every effort to do? What does it mean to "keep the unity" with other Christians?

Ephesians 4:1-6

Ephesians 4:2,3 tells us good ways to treat each other. Which do you think is hardest for most people to do? Why?

Ephesians 4:1-6

Read Ephesians 4:3. Why do you think people who follow Jesus need to have unity or work together?

Ephesians 4:1-6

What are some examples of ways we can obey the instructions in Ephesians 4:2?

Ephesians 4:1-6

In Ephesians 4:4, Paul used the word "body" to describe the Church, or the group of people who follow Jesus. How is a church like a body?

Ephesians 4:1-6

Answering the Questions
Discussion Cards - Ephesians 4:29–5:1

If everyone followed the instructions of Ephesians 4:29, what change would you notice in your favorite TV show? Your friends at school? Your family? Yourself?

Ephesians 4:29–5:1

What advice does Ephesians 4:29–5:1 give us about how to treat others when we're angry or when someone is angry with us?

Ephesians 4:29–5:1

Ephesians 4:29 tells us not to let "unwholesome talk come out of [our] mouths." How would getting rid of "unwholesome talk" help stop some of the behaviors mentioned in verse 31?

Ephesians 4:29–5:1

How would you say Ephesians 4:31 in your own words?

Ephesians 4:29–5:1

Ephesians 4:29 tells us we should say things that "build others up." What good things can happen when we use kind and encouraging words? What are some examples of words that "build others up"?

Ephesians 4:29–5:1

The word "slander" in Ephesians 4:31 means unkind lies that hurt a person's feelings and reputation. What can you do when you feel like saying unkind things about other people?

Ephesians 4:29–5:1

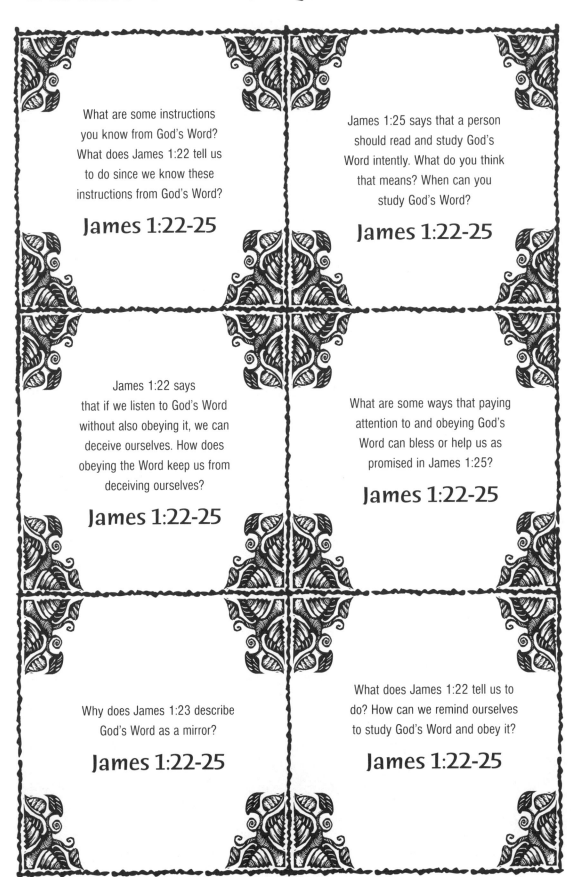

What are some instructions you know from God's Word? What does James 1:22 tell us to do since we know these instructions from God's Word?

James 1:22-25

James 1:25 says that a person should read and study God's Word intently. What do you think that means? When can you study God's Word?

James 1:22-25

James 1:22 says that if we listen to God's Word without also obeying it, we can deceive ourselves. How does obeying the Word keep us from deceiving ourselves?

James 1:22-25

What are some ways that paying attention to and obeying God's Word can bless or help us as promised in James 1:25?

James 1:22-25

Why does James 1:23 describe God's Word as a mirror?

James 1:22-25

What does James 1:22 tell us to do? How can we remind ourselves to study God's Word and obey it?

James 1:22-25

Discussion Cards • 1 John 3:16-18

How does 1 John 3:16 describe God's love? How did Jesus lay down His life? How can we "lay down our lives" to show love to others?

1 John 3:16-18

What situation is described in 1 John 3:17? Why do you think it is important to not just claim to love other people but also show love with our actions?

1 John 3:16-18

What example does 1 John 3:17 give as a way to show God's love? What are some other ways to show God's love?

1 John 3:16-18

Based on 1 John 3:16-18, how would you define what it means to truly show God's love to someone?

1 John 3:16-18

How can you show the kind of love described in 1 John 3:16-18 to a person who feels lonely? Who is sick? Who needs to know about Jesus?

1 John 3:16-18

What does 1 John 3:17 tell us to do with our material possessions? What are some things that you can share with others? Who do you know who might need something you could share?

1 John 3:16-18

Drawing a Picture

Ads for an Ark and More

Goal: To have fun and think creatively about some of the objects in the Bible.

What Do I Need?

- Paper
- Crayons or markers
- Samples of ads from magazines

How Do I Do It?

- Hand out paper and crayons or markers to children.
- Assign each child one of the objects from the Bible that is listed below or have all the children create an ad for the same object.
- Tell children to draw advertisements for the objects.
- Ask teachers to walk around and help children with spelling, etc. Teachers could also supply ideas for those children who are having trouble thinking of ads.

Bricks for the Tower of Babel
Wood for an ark (Noah)
Feed for animals in the ark (Noah)
A guide book for shepherds (Abraham)
A talking donkey (Balaam)
Multi-colored coats (Joseph)
Waterproof baskets (Moses)
Frog-catching net to help with the
     plague of frogs (Israelites in Egypt)

Fly-swatters (plague of flies in Egypt)
Manna cookbook (Moses and Israelites)
Map to the Promised Land (Moses and
     Israelites)
Quail cookbook (Moses and Israelites)
Harp (David)
Seasick medicine (Jonah)
Sycamore trees (hints for climbing by
     Zacchaeus)
Tents (made by Paul)

Take It Another Step

Display the ads where they can be enjoyed by the adults in your church.

Drawing a Picture
Colorful Creativity

Goal: To have fun and think creatively about some different subjects in the Bible and at church.

What Do I Need?
- Paper (thin paper or tissue paper for A Different Perspective)
- Crayons or markers

Lines and Circles
- On each paper draw a line. The line may be squiggly or straight, long or short. You may draw different-sized lines or the same size line on each paper. Circles, ovals, rectangles or triangles are also options.
- Hand out paper, markers or crayons to the children. Tell children to draw a scene from a Bible story using the shape on the paper as part of their drawing.
- Have children talk about their pictures.

Our Church
- Hand out paper, markers and crayons to the children.
- Tell each child to draw a picture of what he or she thinks your church will look like in 20 years.
- If children are having difficulty getting started, ask questions such as, "If you're drawing the outside of the church, do you think the trees will be taller? What do you think our sign will say? Do you think the church building will be bigger? If you're drawing the inside, do you think there will be new technology? Do you think the auditorium will be bigger?"
- Ask children to talk about their pictures.

Our Room
- Hand out paper, markers and crayons to the children.
- Ask the children: Imagine you are on a TV decorating show and your job is to redo our classroom. What would you do?
- When children are done, allow them to show their pictures to the class.
- Pay attention to what they've done. They might have some good ideas that you actually could do.

A Different Perspective
- Hand out paper and crayons. (If you have a class of older children, you could use white tissue paper.)
- Tell children to go around the room and do crayon rubbings of different objects: tile floor, wall, piano keys, chairs, door, etc. (You may have to explain to younger children how to do a rubbing.) (If the weather is appropriate, take the class outside and do rubbings of tree bark, sidewalks, bricks etc.)
- Take the final rubbings and make a collage. Display it in your room.

Take It Another Step
Label the pictures and display them where they can be enjoyed by the adults in your church.

Drawing a Picture
Map Making

Goal: To have fun and think about ways to help the people in your neighborhood.

What Do I Need?

- Two lengths of butcher paper, newsprint, tablecloth paper, etc.
- Markers

How Do I Do It?

- Before you do this as a class project, familiarize yourself with the church neighborhood.
- Divide class into two groups.
- Give each group a long length of paper. Tell one group to imagine they are turning right out of the church parking lot and the other group that they are turning left. They are to draw a picture of the street, including businesses, houses along the street, cross streets, fields, parks, etc. (It's OK if students are not able to label streets.)
- Put the two large pictures together to make one long street and hang on your wall.
- Talk about the picture being your mission field. Brainstorm ways your church can be missionaries to the neighborhood. If any of the children come up with unusual ideas, you might want to pass them along to your pastor or church mission's team.

Take It Another Step

Each week as you see the picture, invite children to pray with you for the people in your neighborhood.

Drawing a Picture
Our Class Book

Goal: To have fun and design a class yearbook.

What Do I Need?

- Paper
- Crayons or markers
- Digital camera(s)

How Do I Do It?

This will be an ongoing art project. To begin, lead children to brainstorm plans for the book, and then continue taking pictures, etc. during future weeks.

- Explain to the children you would like them to make a book titled: *A Visit to Our Class.*
- List the different activities you do in your class.
- Allow children to take pictures of those activities with a digital camera.
- Choose children with good handwriting or printing to write captions on the pages. Or, type captions into the computer and then print it out. (If you have a print shop capability, do the entire book on the computer. Add music and give each child his or her own CD of the final result.)

Take It Another Step

If your book isn't too big, make copies for each child.

Drawing a Picture
Quilting Bee

Goal: To design a wall quilt and review Bible verses.

What Do I Need?

- Bibles
- Different colored construction paper cut in large squares
- Crayons or markers

How Do I Do It?

- Tell the children to think of their favorite Bible verses.
- Have the children draw pictures that illustrates words or concepts in the verses. (Optional: Children write key phrases from verses on squares.)
- Collect the completed pictures.
- During the week, staple the pictures together along with blank squares to form a paper quilt.
- You may wish to staple a paper border around the edges of the quilt. Make narrow cuts in the border to look like a fringe.
- Hang the completed quilt in your room.

Take It Another Step

Give your paper quilt to a staff member or special teacher.

Ending the Story

Goal: To encourage children to think about the decisions they make in their everyday lives. (Note: Some stories may bring up difficult life situations. Talk to your supervisor if a child reveals information that indicates the child is being treated inappropriately.)

What Do I Need?

- Choose a story from pages 38-48. Make a copy of the story for each child.
- Paper, whiteboard, chalkboard or poster board for children to write their endings.

How Do I Do It?

- Give each child a copy of the chosen story to read. Read, or ask a good reader, to read the story aloud.
- Give the children opportunity to finish the story by suggesting several possible endings to the story. Teachers or students write suggested endings on paper, whiteboard, chalkboard or poster board. (You could do this in one large group, in small groups or individually.)
- Come together in a large group. Children take turns telling possible endings to the story and then vote on their favorite ending.
- Use the Discussion Questions at the end of each story to discuss the story and possible endings. Use the verses listed (or other verses of your choice) to guide children toward a biblically-based answer.

Take It Another Step

Ask children to volunteer stories of situations when they didn't know what to do. Allow other children to offer possible solutions. Always summarize with a biblically-based answer.

Ending the Story
Free Coupons

Here was Dylan's chance. His dad was outside mowing the lawn. His mom was busy making supper. Even his pesky little brother was busy annoying the dog.

"Carter," Dylan whispered to his friend. "Come here, I gotta show you something cool."

Carter got up from the floor. He and Dylan had been drawing elaborate diagrams of football plays. "What?"

"Just come here."

"It's not bad . . . is it?" Carter sounded unsure. Dylan usually yelled stuff. He wouldn't whisper unless he had something to hide.

"Of course not. It's cool." Dylan sat down at the computer and quickly went to the Internet.

"You sure this isn't bad?" Carter asked.

Dylan clicked on a link. "No way. Look it's just the site for the Game Shed."

"Oh, yeah, I ALREADY know about THAT." Carter sounded relieved. "They have that special online coupon for $5.00 worth of tokens. My brother printed one of those last week."

"Yeah, but watch this." Dylan messed around clicking some more buttons. "I figured out how to get an endless supply."

Carter headed back to the football diagrams. "They all have numbers on them, silly. You can't just print off 20 coupons. They even say each number is used only once."

"Nope. I tricked the system. Each one I print has a different number. I can use like five or six of these at one time. I'll just tell them other people gave them to me."

"There's something not right about that, Dylan."

"Yeah, whatever, Carter. You can't find one thing wrong about what I did. I wasn't trying to beat the system, it just happened. So, it's their mistake, not mine."

"Still . . . "

Discussion Questions

- If Dylan didn't think he was wrong, why did he wait until his parents were busy to show Carter the coupons?
- Is it wrong to do something that doesn't follow the rules? Why?
- What additional problem happens when Dylan takes five coupons to the Game Shed and says that other people gave them to him? (Even if he gets away with it, he's lied.)
- Read Proverbs 12:22, Ephesians 4:25 and Philippians 4:8. What do these verses tell us about how to act in this situation?

Ending the Story
The Lady Next Door

"Life gets no better than this!" Justin Donahue jumped down the porch steps and then turned around to wait for his brother. "After Uncle Steve pays us for raking his yard I'll have enough money for Wacky World—the computer game of my dreams!"

"Not quite," Jonathan reminded him. "Don't forget tax. You'll need about another five dollars."

Justin stared at his brother. "Really? I forgot about that." Then he brightened again. "No problem. You can loan me the money."

"Not on your life, little bro. I'm saving mine for a new snowboard and I WILL have enough. Dad's taking me to the sporting goods store tonight."

"How come you get . . . "

"Boys, boys, come here a minute," Mrs. Jefferson, the elderly lady who lived next door, motioned to them from her porch.

"Wonder what this is about?" Justin whispered. Jonathan shrugged.

Mrs. Jefferson had lived by herself as long as Justin and Jonathan could remember. Her husband had died and her son and daughter lived across the country. They never came to see her. Sometimes Jonathan and Justin would help her do some things around her house and she always made them great peanut butter cookies in return. But she didn't have much money and Mr. Donahue had told the boys a long time ago that helping Mrs. Jefferson was a way of serving the Lord.

Now, they followed Mrs. Jefferson into the house. "You boys can go into the kitchen." She smiled her sweet, old-lady smile. "I just took some cookies out of the oven." She shuffled off down the hall. "I was cleaning out Paul's closet and came across a box that I might as well give to you two."

"Box of what?" Justin whispered to Jonathan as they attacked the plateful of warm cookies.

"Box of spiders?" Jonathan laughed.

"Nails?" Justin guessed.

"Mice?"

"Moldy cheese?"

The boys stopped their silly guessing as Mrs. Jefferson walked into the kitchen and put a shoebox on the table. "Just take them. Paul hasn't been to visit me in years and I'm trying to get rid of some stuff. I'll probably have to go into a nursing home soon." She smiled sadly. "That's life, boys. I'll miss your family, though. You're nice people."

Jonathan knew he should say something because Mrs. Jefferson was nice, too, but he felt kind of embarrassed, so he finally said, "We'll miss your cookies, Mrs. Jefferson. They're the best."

"Yeah," Justin agreed, but he couldn't say much else because at the moment his mouth was full of cookies.

The boys said good-bye, took the box and left. Jonathan ran the box home and then the boys went down the street to rake Uncle Steve's yard.

39

Later that evening Justin remembered the box. "Probably nothing," Jonathan said as he opened the lid.

But it was something.

Inside were stamps. Lots of them.

Jonathan dumped some out on the table.

"What do you have there?" Mr. Donahue walked into the room.

"Stamps," Justin said. "Mrs. Jefferson gave them to us."

"I guess Paul used to collect them before he moved away," Jonathan added.

Mr. Donahue picked up a see-through plastic envelope with a stamp inside. He studied it a minute and then picked up another one. He suddenly turned serious and got a funny look on his face. "My dad used to collect stamps so I know a little about them. I think some of these are worth money. Paul sure didn't just get them at a hobby store in one of those 500 for $5.00 deals."

"But they're ours now, right Dad?" Justin picked up a light green, three-cent stamp. "We get to keep them."

Mr. Donahue shook his head. "Are you sure Mrs. Jefferson knew she was giving you something of value? We know she's struggling financially."

"But Dad," Jonathan said. "She DID give them to us. We didn't ask for them. If they're worth a lot of money, would we have to give them back?"

Mr. Donahue put his hand on Jonathan's shoulder, "What do you think?"

Discussion Questions

- Mrs. Jefferson gave the boys the box of stamps. When might returning the gift be the right thing to do?
- Do you think Mrs. Jefferson knew the value of the stamps? Why or why not?
- What could the boys do with the stamps? (Take them to a stamp store and find out how much they're worth. If they're worth a lot, maybe the boys should give them back or at least split the value with her.)
- Why might the boys feel they had a right to keep the stamps?
- Read Galatians 6:2, Philippians 2:3 and 1 Timothy 5:1-2. What do these verses tell us about how to act in this situation?

Ending the Story
The Look Book

"Hey, Myles," Sam called as soon as Myles walked in the classroom door.

"I was on the Internet last night and saw you got your page up on Look Book. Cool!"

"Look Book? My mom won't let me near that site." Kelli shook her head. "She says some of that stuff is really bad."

"Look Book isn't like those sites for teenagers, Kel. They tell you on their advertisement: 'Look at the book that's just for kids,'" Myles defended.

"Still." Kelli shrugged. "Anyone can get on there and read about you. Mom says some of the people have wrong motives. She's read that their security system doesn't work."

"Yeah, and your mom wouldn't let you go to that movie last week either. YOU can't do ANYTHING," Sam told her. "Look Book is perfectly OK."

"Oh!" Sam suddenly yelled. "I left my homework in my locker." He headed out the door.

"To tell you the truth," Myles confessed after Sam was gone. "My parents told me I couldn't do a page on Look Book either. But I decided to do one anyhow. When I show my parents how careful I've been with my personal information, I think they'll be OK with it."

"But Sam, aren't you disobeying your parents? Don't you think they have their reasons for telling you to stay off the site?"

"Well, sure, but . . . ."

Discussion Questions

- Who is right and who is wrong in this story? Why?
- What were the choices these kids had to make?
- Is Myles wrong because he created a page on Look Book (a fictitious site) or because he disobeyed his parents?
- What are some guidelines to follow when you are online? How can you learn more about what web sites are safe for kids to use?
- Read Ephesians 6:1. What does this verse tell us about how to act in this situation?

Ending the Story
Just Down the Street

"Mom, I'm leaving," Belinda got her jacket out of her closet. "I should be back by supper."

"OK." Her mom walked into the hallway. "You and Elizabeth make sure to get that project done. I don't want you leaving her house. You need to work and I don't want you walking around the neighborhood without me knowing where you are."

"I know. I know. We'll get it done. Do you know the exact date the Revolutionary War started, Mom?"

Belinda's mom laughed. "Good. You're actually learning stuff while you're working. Now, remember, I don't want you leaving Elizabeth's house."

Belinda carefully walked down the porch steps. She was carrying poster board, markers, pictures, clay and at least seven other things necessary for her and Elizabeth to finish their Revolutionary War project.

She hoped no one was watching as she walked up the street to Elizabeth's house. She was sure she looked silly balancing all that stuff, but fortunately Elizabeth lived just three houses away and was waiting for her by the door.

The girls quickly sat down to work. They molded a landscape from the clay and Elizabeth contributed some small plastic soldiers from her brother's collection.

"This is looking really cool," Belinda said. "You think we'll get an 'A'?"

"Hoping." Elizabeth suddenly jumped up. "Hey, my grandma has some small stones in her driveway. Let's run over and get some and we can make paths in our fields."

"Mom told me I couldn't leave the house."

Elizabeth rolled her eyes. "Belinda, my grandmother lives two blocks away. We can cut through the Johnson's yard and be there in three minutes. What's the big deal?"

"My mom said I couldn't leave the house. That's what the big deal is."

"So call her," Elizabeth said, but Belinda was already on the way to the phone.

The phone was busy.

"Belinda. Come on. It's not like we're going to the store or to someone else's house. The stones are FOR the project."

"I know, but . . . ."

Discussion Questions

- What choice did Belinda have to make?
- Why might Belinda think it would be OK to go to the grandmother's house?
- What do you think Belinda's mother would want her to do? Why?
- What could Belinda do in this situation to show that she wanted to obey her mother?
- Read Ephesians 6:1. What does this verse tell us about how to act in this situation?

Ending the Story
Game Tickets

Nathan slapped an envelope down on Derek's desk. "In there is your ticket for Friday's game."

"Friday's game?" Derek stared at his friend. "What game?"

"THE game. My dad got the tickets from some guy at work. He said we'd pick you up at four o'clock."

Derek jumped up and gave Nathan three high fives. "NO one has tickets for Friday's game. No way."

"My dad got them from some guy at work. He has season tickets, but now has to go to on a business trip or something. Anyhow, Dad said he'd call your parents about all the arrangements."

Derek could NOT believe he had a ticket to the biggest game of the year. He didn't pay attention to anything at school that day. And after school, he ran the entire five blocks home and burst into the house. "Mom, you'll NEVER believe it! NEVER! Nathan's dad got me a ticket for Friday night's game."

"I heard. I just got off the phone with him."

"Whoa! Isn't this the coolest thing ever?" Derek flopped on the couch. "I can't believe it. This Friday night . . . ."

"Is the night of Great Grandma Louise's ninetieth birthday party," his mom reminded him.

"But Mom . . . ."

"But Derek, our family has been planning this for a year. Everyone will be there. Even Uncle Bill is flying in from London. You haven't seen him since you were a baby. And Great Grandma Louise has always been special to you. You even stayed with her when you were a toddler and I was in the hospital having your sister."

"I know. I know." Derek banged the couch in frustration. "Why couldn't the party be some other night?"

"What's going on?" Derek's dad walked in the door. Derek's mom explained what was happening with the game and the party.

"Do I HAVE to go to the party?" Derek asked. "I might never, ever have a chance to go to a game like this again."

Derek watched as his dad and mom gave each other one of those looks that told Derek they each knew what the other one was thinking.

"I understand how important the game is to you," his father said. "I also know that Great Grandma Louise would want you at her party. The choice is up to you as to which one you go to."

"Me?" Derek jumped off the couch. "Why me?"

Life would be so much easier if his parents just said "yes" or "no."

Discussion Questions

- What would you choose to do in this situation? Why?
- What does Derek need to think about in making this decision? (He may never have an opportunity to go to such an important game again. He wouldn't have an opportunity to celebrate his great-grandmother's ninetieth birthday again. The value of people compared to the value of games.)
- Read Proverbs 17:6, Romans 12:10 and Philippians 2:3. What do these verses tell us about how to act in this situation?

Ending the Story
DVD Decision

"Hey, my dad's back. Come on, Jacob." Cody dashed down the steps and Jacob followed. "He said he'd stop at the video store for us and get some DVDs." Cody opened the door to let his dad in from the cold air.

"You get something good, Dad?"

Mr. Anderson took off his coat. "Sure did. They actually had Dark Flyers."

"Fantastic! We've been waiting for that one forever." Cody grabbed the DVD and hurried into the other room.

Mr. Anderson walked into the kitchen. "Don't start it yet, Cody. I'll make some popcorn and watch it with you."

"Is this cool or what, Jacob?" Cody stuck the DVD into the player. "Have you seen Dark Flyers yet?"

"No." Jacob's answer wasn't very loud, but Cody didn't seem to notice.

Jacob walked over to the window and stared at the cars passing in the street. What should he do? He knew his parents didn't want him watching Dark Flyers, but his parents were in Atlanta for a wedding and he wasn't supposed to call on the cell phone unless there was an emergency. A DVD wasn't an emergency, was it?

Besides, the Andersons went to the same church as Jacob and his family. Mr. Anderson was a Sunday School teacher. He wouldn't be showing the boys something they shouldn't see, would he?

Still, Jacob knew that his parents didn't want him to see Dark Flyers.

Maybe I could sit in Cody's room and play on his computer, Jacob thought. But he knew Cody would ask what was wrong. Yet, he didn't want to offend Mr. Anderson by saying his parents wouldn't like his choice.

Jacob sighed. What a mess!

Discussion Questions

- What options did Jacob have? (Call his parents if he was sure they weren't in the middle of the wedding. Tell Mr. Anderson what he was worried about. Not watch the DVD.)
- What would be the easiest choice to make? The hardest? What might the consequences be of each choice?
- Read Ephesians 6:10, Philippians 4:7-8 and 1 Timothy 6:11. What do these verses tell us about how to act in this situation?

Ending the Story
You Didn't Hear That

"Unbelievable!" Cindy gave Emma a high five. "I did it! I solved the crime." She hit pause. "This computer game is awesome, Emma. I'll have to ask my parents if I can get one."

Emma shrugged. "You can borrow mine if you want. I've done all the levels."

"Could I? I want to show my dad and . . . ."

Cindy's voice trailed off as they heard a loud crash downstairs.

"You jerk!" A man's voice shook the house.

"Stop it! Just stop it!" A lady sobbed.

At first Cindy thought someone had turned on the TV, but then she realized she was listening to Emma's parents. She looked at her friend. "Emma?"

"They always do this." Tears ran down Emma's face. "They're thinking about getting a divorce."

Cindy didn't know what to say. Emma's parents getting a divorce? Her parents were so nice. At least that's what Cindy had always thought. But listening to the yelling and banging downstairs, she wasn't so sure.

"Sometimes my dad even hits my mom." Emma's voice was so quiet, Cindy could hardly hear her.

"Does anyone else know about this?" Cindy asked.

"Oh, Cindy, no! You can't tell anyone. You gotta promise. Please. Please, promise? You just can't tell a soul."

Cindy didn't know what to do.

Discussion Questions

Some of the boys and girls in your class may be going through similar experiences. Talking about fictional characters may encourage them to get their thoughts out in the open.

- Should Cindy promise not to tell? Why or why not?
- Who might be trustworthy adults Cindy could talk to? (Parents, grandparents, teachers or pastors at church, etc.)
- Even if friends have promised NOT to tell secrets, when would it be OK to break that promise? (When someone is getting hurt and needs help.)
- Read Proverbs 17:17, Romans 12:10 and Ephesians 4:32. What do these verses tell us about how to act in this situation?

45

Ending the Story
Sing a Song!

Chloe and Samantha hurried into the community center. Today Miss Larsen would tell them the songs they would be singing at the Town Spring Festival. Yesterday she told the group she had found some with funny lyrics. All the kids were excited. They would be singing in the county auditorium and thousands of people would be there to hear them. Cool!

"Who do you think she'll pick for the solo parts?" Chloe asked Samantha. "I mean, that would be so cool! Maybe some big producer will be there, and he'd want us to do our own CD and . . . ."

Sam laughed. "Chloe, we're only 11 years old. No producer is going to be listening to us, trying to find the next big star. I just hope it doesn't rain. It's rained the past five festival weekends."

The girls took their seats as Miss Larsen began the rehearsal.

Chloe listened. She knew the first two songs—and she DID like them. She kind of knew the next one, too, but she didn't know the last one at all.

Miss Larsen played the music and then gave each of them a sheet with the words of the lyrics. "By next week, I want these lyrics memorized," she told the group.

A couple of the kids groaned, but Chloe was busy reading down through the lyrics. Everything was fine until she got to the song she didn't know—right in the middle was a bad word—a word she wasn't allowed to say.

"Sam," she whispered. "Look at the last line." She pointed to the word.

"Chloe." Miss Larsen sounded angry. "Please listen. I am giving instructions you need to know."

"Yes, Miss Larsen," Chloe said, but she felt funny inside. She knew that it was a really bad word. Why would Miss Larsen make them sing it?

"Lord, give me courage," she prayed silently. After class she went up to the teacher even though she had a million somersaulting butterflies in her stomach.

"Yes, Chloe?"

"Miss Larsen," Chloe said pointing to the word. "I don't want to sing this."

Miss Larsen gave her a strange look. "Why not? It's an important part of the song."

"But it's not right. It's using God's name in a wrong way."

Miss Larsen laughed. "Here's your choice, Chloe. You sing or you don't get to be in the performance."

"But I . . . ."

Discussion Questions

- Does it make a difference that the word is part of the song? Why or why not?
- If Chloe decided that singing the word is wrong, what could she do next?
- Who could Chloe ask to help her know what to do? (Pray to God. Talk to her parents.)
- Read Exodus 20:7 and Deuteronomy 5:11. What do these verses tell us about how to act in this situation?

Brother Trouble—Younger Elementary

Molly and Shawna were lying on Shawna's floor, painting frogs and butterflies with Shawna's new watercolor set.

"Maybe I'll save my picture and give it to my mom for her birthday." Molly studied her purple, blue and pink butterfly.

"That's a good idea. My . . . ."

Shawna's little brother exploded into the room. "Whacha girls doing?"

"Get out, Thomas." Shawna picked her paper up from the floor. "We're painting. No boys allowed."

"I want to paint." Thomas sat down on the floor and reached for a brush.

"You're too young," Shawna said.

"I'm THREE." Thomas smiled.

"I KNOW you're three, but that's too young to use my new paints. Now get out of here."

"I want to paint." Thomas started sniffing like he was going to cry.

"You can't," Shawna said again. Then suddenly she got a mean look on her face.

"You know why you can't stay in here and paint, Thomas?"

"Why?"

"Because there's a big monster under my bed. He has green eyes and red and orange pointy things on him. He likes girls, but he eats little boys."

Thomas' eyes got wider and wider as Shawna talked.

"You'd better get going," Shawna said. "I wouldn't want him to hear you. That would make him come out of there and gobble you up before you had a chance to move."

Thomas crawled to his feet and ran out the door.

"And that is that," Shawna said.

"And that wasn't very nice," Molly started on a flowered border on her paper.

Shawna shrugged. "He's not supposed to be in here. I didn't tell him it was true. I mean, we both know it was just pretend. What's wrong with it?"

Discussion Questions
- Should Shawna have told her brother there was a monster under the bed? Why or why not?
- What could Shawna have done?
- What are some good things Shawna could do now? (Apologize to her brother. Show him that there aren't monsters under the bed. Do an art project with him.)
- Read Proverbs 26:18-19 and Ephesians 4:25. What do these verses tell us about how to act in this situation?

Ending the Story
Clean-Up Duty—Younger Elementary

"Dad, Mom, is it time to leave for Grandma's?" Micah ran into the kitchen. "You said two o'clock and it's almost two."

Mr. Mulligan shook his head. "Sorry, Micah. We won't be able to leave for awhile. That was Pastor Jeff on the phone. He and the people who usually clean the church have to go to a funeral. He asked if Mom and I could clean the church for tomorrow. Of course, I said 'yes.' We'll have to wait until we're done before we can leave."

Micah would've stomped his foot on the floor, but he knew that would just get him into trouble. "I don't understand why WE have to do it. We have somewhere to go, too."

"That's true, but going to Grandma's house for a fun visit isn't as important as a funeral. Besides, we'll still have plenty of time after we clean the church. In fact, get your stuff ready and we'll be on our way."

Micah wasn't any happier once they got to church. His dad handed him a dust rag and told him to dust off the chairs in the Sunday School rooms. That was fine until he came to a big wad of gum stuck on one of the seats.

"I can't get this off," he called to his mom.

His mom came in and looked at the gum. "Who would do something like this?" She wasn't really asking, just talking to herself. "It's your classroom, Micah."

"Yeah, and last Sunday . . . ."

Oops! Micah realize that's where HE HAD been sitting. His friend had given him the gum and after he was done chewing it, HE HAD stuck it on the chair.

Getting the gum off took a lot of time, but finally they just had the auditorium left to do.

"Micah, Mom will dust and I'll vacuum. Pick up the papers in the pews."

Micah walked down one row and then the other, picking up bulletins and used tissues (yuck) and candy wrappers and putting then in a trash bag. Then he came to a row with bunches of little pieces of paper everywhere.

"Oh, no," Micah mumbled. He remembered that he and his friends had been seeing who could tear up their children's bulletin into the most pieces. That was HIS mess.

"What's taking you so long, Micah?" his dad asked.

Discussion Questions

- After this story, how might Micah's behavior at church change? Why?
- What are some ways we all can help to keep our church building looking good?
- Read 1 Corinthians 12:12-23. What do these verses tell us about how to act in this situation? (It's important to work together to get the job done. If we do our part in keeping the church clean, then other people won't have to work so hard. Taking good care of the church furniture and carpet saves the church money. That money can then be used for other purposes.)

Figuring It Out

Goal: For children to practice looking verses up in the Bible—and have fun figuring out the problem.

What Do I Need?

- Bibles
- Paper and pencils, whiteboard or chalkboard
- One of the Figuring It Out activities on pages 52-55 and Answer Key on pages 50-51

How Do I Do It?

- You can do this as an individual or group activity. For a group activity, choose children to take turns reading the math problems, looking up and reading the Bible verses, calculating the numbers and writing the answers on the whiteboard or chalkboard. Or, you can divide the children into small groups and have the groups race against each other to see which group first comes up with the correct answer. (Make sure you mix kids with math ability with those who are younger or who aren't as quick with figures so that the groups are evenly divided.)
- Since some children will know final answers (such as how many disciples there are), tell them they have to tell you all the numbers to all the steps of the math problem BEFORE they are declared the winner.

Figuring It Out
Answer Key

Bible Activity #1

1. Begin with 6 days (Genesis 1:31) 6
2. Add 123 years (Numbers 33:39) 129
3. Subtract 29 years (2 Chronicles 25:1) 100
4. Divide by Ten Commandments (Exodus 34:28) .10
5. Add 600,000 men (Exodus 12:37) 600,010
6. Subtract 10 brothers (Genesis 42:3) 600,000
7. Divide by 6 years (Exodus 23:10) 100,000
8. Subtract 50,000 drachmas (Acts 19:19) 50,000
9. Divide by 50 cubits (Exodus 27:13) 1,000
10. Subtract by 1,000 years (Psalm 90:4) 0

Answer: 0

Bible Activity #2

1. Begin with 10 shekels (Genesis 24:22) 10
2. Add 70 elders (Numbers 11:24) 80
3. Subtract 40 years (Numbers 32:13) 40
4. Add 1 place (Genesis 1:9) 41
5. Multiply by 2 lights (Genesis 1:16) 82
6. Add 1,000 goats (1 Samuel 25:2) 1082
7. Subtract 300 shekels (Genesis 45:22) 782
8. Subtract 700 men (Judges 20:15) 82
9. Subtract 20 years twice (40) (2 Chronicles 28:1) 42
10. Subtract 2 years (Acts 28:30) 40

Answer: 40 (Forty days, Genesis 7:12)

Bible Activity #3

1. Begin with 6 years (Judges 12:7) 6
2. Add 1 son (Genesis 10:25) 7
3. Subtract 4 anchors (Acts 27:29) 3
4. Add 15 sons (2 Samuel 9:10) 18
5. Subtract 8 years (Acts 9:33) 10
6. Subtract 5 loaves (John 6:9) 5
7. Add 3 sons (Genesis 9:19) 8
8. Subtract 4 things (Proverbs 30:18) 4
9. Add 6 days (Exodus 31:15) 10
10. Add 2 chains (Exodus 28:14) 12

Answer: 12 (Matthew 11:1)

Bible Activity #4

1. Begin with 100 years (Genesis 17:17) 100
2. Add 900 chariots (Judges 4:3) 1000
3. Subtract 40 years (Genesis 25:20) 960

4. Multiply by 2 years (Genesis 45:6) 1920
5. Subtract 1,000 hills (Psalm 50:10) 920
6. Divide by five posts (Exodus 36:38) 184
7. Subtract 180 years (Genesis 35:28) 4
8. Multiply by 8 sons (1 Samuel 17:12) 32
9. Add 30 days (Daniel 6:12) 62
10. Add 4 men (Daniel 3:25) 66

Answer: 66

Bible Activity #5

1. Begin with 20 rams (Genesis 32:14) 20
2. Add 300 trumpets (Judges 7:22) 320
3. Divide by 8 men (Jeremiah 41:15) 40
4. Multiply by 4 days (Acts 10:30) 160
5. Add 40 years (1 Ezekiel 29:13) 200
6. Divide by 2 men (1 Samuel 10:2) 100
7. Subtract by 50 years (John 8:57) 50
8. Subtract the 13 cities (Joshua 21:19) 37
9. Subtract 30 years (Luke 3:23) 7
10. Subtract 6 years (Leviticus 25:3) 6

Answer: 1 (John 14:6)

Bible Activity #6

1. Begin with 18 men (Ezra 8:18) 18
2. Add 10 days (Genesis 24:55) 28
3. Divide by 7 churches (Revelation 1:4) 4
4. Multiply by 7 times (Psalm 119:164) 28
5. Add the 1 thing (Luke 18:22) 29
6. Subtract 15 days (Galatians 1:18) 14
7. Add 4 months (Judges 20:47) 18
8. Add 65 years (Genesis 5:21) 83
9. Multiply by 1,000 years (Psalm 90:4) 83,000
10. Add 300 trumpets (Judges 7:22) 83,300

Answer: 83,300

Bible Activity #7

1. Begin with number of the child's choosing
2. Add 40 years (Numbers 14:34)
3. Add 2 books (1 and 2 Samuel)
4. Child subtracts original number.
5. Add 12 spies (Numbers 13:3-17) 54
6. Add 2 spies (Numbers 14:6-9) 56
7. Divide by 7 days.

Answer: 8

Figuring It Out
Bible Activity #1

Figure Out the Following Math Problem:

1. Begin with the number of days God used to create the earth. (Genesis 1:31)
2. Add that to age of Aaron when he died. (Numbers 33:39)
3. Subtract the number of years King Amaziah reigned in Jerusalem. (2 Chronicles 25:1)
4. Divide by the number of Commandments. (Exodus 34:28)
5. Add the number of Israelite men who traveled to Rameses on foot. (Exodus 12:37)
6. Subtract the number of Joseph's brothers who went down to Egypt. (Genesis 42:3)
7. Divide by the number of years you sow your fields. (Exodus 23:10)
8. Subtract the value of the scrolls. (Acts 19:19)
9. Divide by the width of the courtyard. (Exodus 27:13)
10. Subtract the number of years a day is in God's sight. (Psalm 90:4)

Your answer should equal the number of funny-looking people in the room!

Bible Activity #2

Figure Out the Following Math Problem:

1. Begin with the weight of the two gold bracelets. (Genesis 24:22)
2. Add that to the number of elders. (Numbers 11:24)
3. Subtract the number of years the Israelites wandered in the wilderness. (Numbers 32:13)
4. Add the number of places where God gathered the water. (Genesis 1:9)
5. Multiply by the number of great lights God made. (Genesis 1:16)
6. Add the number of goats Nabal (the rich man) had. (1 Samuel 25:2)
7. Subtract the number of pieces of silver given to Benjamin. (Genesis 45:22)
8. Subtract the number of chosen men. (Judges 20:15)
9. Subtract the age of Ahaz TWICE. (2 Chronicles 28:1)
10. Subtract the number of years Paul stayed in the rented house. (Acts 28:30)

Your answer should equal the number days rain flooded the earth while Noah and his family were safe in the ark. (Genesis 7:12)

Bible Activity #3

Figure Out the Following Math Problem:

1. Begin with the number of years Jephthah judged Israel. (Judges 12:7)
2. Add the number of sons named Peleg. (Genesis 10:25)
3. Subtract the number of anchors. (Acts 27:29)
4. Add the number of Ziba's sons. (2 Samuel 9:10)
5. Subtract the number of years the man was in bed. (Acts 9:33)
6. Subtract the number of loaves the boy had. (John 6:9)
7. Add the sons of Noah. (Genesis 9:19)
8. Subtract the number of things the writer didn't know. (Proverbs 30:18)
9. Add how many days work is to be done. (Exodus 31:15)
10. Add the number of chains of braided gold. (Exodus 28:14)

Your answer should equal the number of disciples. (Matthew 11:1)

Bible Activity #4

Figure Out the Following Math Problem:

1. Begin with the age of Abraham. (Genesis 17:17)
2. Add the number of chariots. (Judges 4:3)
3. Subtract the age of Isaac when he married Rebekah. (Genesis 25:20)
4. Multiply by the number of years famine had already been in the land. (Genesis 45:6).
5. Subtract the number of hills the cattle are on. (Psalm 50:10)
6. Divide by the number of posts. (Exodus 36:38)
7. Subtract the number of years Isaac lived. (Genesis 35:28)
8. Multiply by the number of Jesse's sons. (1 Samuel 17:12)
9. Add the number of days the petition was for. (Daniel 6:12)
10. Add the number of men walking in the fire. (Daniel 3:25)

Your answer should equal the number of books of the Bible.

Figuring It Out
Bible Activity #5

Figure Out the Following Math Problem:

1. Begin with the number of rams. (Genesis 32:14)
2. Add the number of trumpets. (Judges 7:22)
3. Divide by the number of men who escaped with Ishmael. (Jeremiah 41:15)
4. Multiply by the number of days it was since Cornelius prayed. (Acts 10:30)
5. Add the number of years until the Egyptians will be gathered. (Ezekiel 29:13)
6. Divide by the number of men met by Rachel's tomb. (1 Samuel 10:2)
7. Subtract the "age" talked about. (John 8:57)
8. Subtract the number of cities for the children of Aaron. (Joshua 21:19)
9. Subtract the age of Jesus when He began His ministry. (Luke 3:23)
10. Subtract the number of years you sow your fields. (Leviticus 25:3)

Your answer should be the number of ways there are to get to heaven. (John 14:6)

Bible Activity #6

Figure Out the Following Math Problem:

1. Begin with the number of men. (Ezra 8:18)
2. Add the number of days. (Genesis 24:55)
3. Divide by the number of churches. (Revelation 1:4)
4. Multiply by the number of times a day the Psalmist praised God. (Psalm 119:164)
5. Add the number of things the man lacked. (Luke 18:22)
6. Subtract the number of days Paul stayed with Peter. (Galatians 1:18)
7. Add the number of months the men stayed in Rimmon. (Judges 20:47)
8. Add the age of Enoch when Methuselah was born. (Genesis 5:21)
9. Multiply by the number of years it takes to make a day in God's sight. (Psalm 90:4)
10. Add the number of trumpets. (Judges 7:22)

Your answer should be the number of times you should smile at your teacher this month!

Bible Activity #7–A Puzzle Within a Puzzle

Figure Out the Following Math Problem:

1. Choose a number from one to ten. Do not tell anyone what number you have chosen.
2. Add the number of years the Israelites wandered in the wilderness. (Numbers 14:34)
3. Add the number of Bible books named Samuel.
4. Subtract your secret number.
5. Add the number of spies sent into the Promised Land. (Numbers 13:3-17)
6. Add the number of spies who were not afraid to enter the Promised Land. (Numbers 14:6-9)
7. Divide by the number of days in a week.

Your answer is 8!

Getting to Know You

Talking It Over

Goal: For you to get to know your children and for the children to get to know each other better.

What Do I Need?

- No supplies needed for this activity

How Do I Do It?

- Sometimes the best thing to do with extra time is to sit in a circle and talk. Ask the kids questions. Listen to their answers. You may be surprised at the insight you get into their lives.

Here are some questions to get you started.

Food

1. What's the yuckiest food you've ever tasted?
2. If you could have dinner with anyone in the world, who would it be? Why?
3. If you could have dinner with anyone in the Bible who would it be? Why? (A good idea with Bible questions is to say "who besides Jesus." Otherwise, "Jesus" will be the common answer.)
4. If you had to eat the same food every day for the next three months, what food would you choose?
5. What vegetable don't you want to eat again?
6. If you owned your own restaurant, what kind of food would you serve? Why?
7. If you were challenged to invent a new kind of pizza, what toppings would you use?
8. What's the best food you've ever tasted?
9. What food would you like to try some day? (Frog legs? Rattlesnake? Alligator?)
10. What's your very favorite meal?

Favorites

1. What is your favorite book?
2. Who is your favorite author?

3. What is your favorite car?
4. What is your favorite movie?
5. Who is your favorite actor or actress?
6. What is your favorite song?
7. Who is your favorite musician?
8. What is your favorite television show?
9. What is your favorite game?
10. What is your favorite Internet site?
11. What is your favorite Bible verse?
12. What is your favorite thing to do on a Saturday?
13. What is your favorite piece of clothing?
14. What is your favorite toy?
15. What is your favorite subject at school?

If Questions

1. If you could live anywhere in the world, where would it be?
2. If you wrote a book, what would it be about?
3. If you invented a machine, what would it do?
4. If you could have an unusual pet, what would it be?
5. If you were president or king, what is the first rule you would make?
6. If you could teach this class, what would you plan for the students to do?
7. If you could see the Bible on DVD, what event would you want to watch?
8. If you could be anyone in the Bible (other than Jesus), who would it be?
9. If you had to play the same sport for 24 hours, what would you play?
10. If you had a million dollars, how would you spend it?
11. If you had the money to start a charity, what would the charity be for?
12. If you could set a world record, what would it be for?
13. If you could do anything you wanted next weekend, what would you do?
14. If you could have chosen your own name, what would we be calling you?
15. If you could be a missionary in another country, what country would you choose and why?

General Questions

1. What was the most exciting thing you did this week?
2. What is the most exciting place you've ever visited?
3. What do you want to be when you're an adult?
4. What's the best gift you've ever received?
5. What talent would you like to have?
6. What time in history would you want to live?
7. What is a good friend like?
8. What is a good teacher like?
9. What is the funniest thing that ever happened to you?
10. What was the happiest moment of your life so far?

Take It Another Step

Allow the children to suggest questions you can ask.

57

Getting to Know You
Do What?

Goal: To encourage children to get to know each other better and to have fun. (Even children who have grown up together in the same church do not always know everything about each other.)

What do I Need?

- No supplies needed for this activity

How Do I Do It?

- Ask the children to sit in a circle. (If you have a large amount of kids, you could divide the group into two sections.)

- The first child stands up, says his or her name and then does an action like snapping fingers, clapping, stomping, singing a line from a song, quoting a Bible verse, jumping, etc.
- The second child stands up, says the first child's name and mimics the action. Then the second child says his or her own name and does a different action.
- The third child then stands up and says the name and does the action of the first and second child, and then adds his or her own name and action.
- Continue until everyone has a turn. Of course, as more and more actions are added, the routine becomes funnier.

Take It Another Step

Discuss how each one of us is different from the other. We are unique people created by God. Read a few verses from Psalm 139 as the foundation for your discussion.

Getting to Know You
Smile

Goal: To encourage children to get to know each other better. (Even children who have grown up together in the same church do not always know each other well.)

What Do I Need?

- Digital camera (more than one, if possible)
- Clear Con-Tact paper or a laminator
- Cardboard or heavy paper to back the pictures.

How Do I Do It?

- Explain to the children that they will not be able to see the end result of this project until another week. Today's goal is getting the project started. (However, if your church has the means of downloading photos, you may be able to complete it in one session.)
- Allow children to take close-up pictures of each other with a child's (extra sturdy) digital camera. These are available from major toy companies. Digital photos don't cost anything to take—so allow for a lot of picture-taking! (Although, it does cost to print them!)

- Choose a good photo of each child and print two copies of each photo. (Approximately 3-inch [7.5-cm] square).
- Attach the pictures onto the heavy paper and cover with clear Con-Tact paper or laminate.

Now, your class has a personalized memory game which can be played over and over.

To play a memory game, turn all pictures face down on a flat surface. Children take turns, turning over two cards at a time. If they make a match, they get to keep those cards and take another turn. If they don't get a match, they turn the cards face down again and the next player takes a turn.

The game is over when all sets are matched. The person (or team) with the most sets is the winner.

Take It Another Step

Discuss how we are all different, yet God is our creator and loves each one of us. Read Genesis 1:26-27 as the foundation for your discussion.

59

Getting to Know You
Find a Seat

Goal: To encourage children to get to know each other better. (Even children who have grown up together in the same church do not always know everything about each other.)

What Do I Need?

- No supplies needed for this activity

How Do I Do It?

- Arrange chairs in a circle. (If you have a large number of kids, you could divide the group into two sections.) Each circle needs one less chair than children. The extra child stands in the center of the circle. (This is a version of Fruit Basket Upset.)
- The center child calls out a category: "Everyone with a brother" or "Everyone who ate pizza for supper last night." The children who fit the category then need to change seats. The center child also rushes to get a seat. Whoever is left without a seat stands in the center for the next round of the game.

Give children the following suggestions:

- Everyone with a sister.
- Everyone whose favorite subject is math.
- Everyone who lives in an apartment.
- Everyone who has a cat.
- Everyone who has a yellow bedroom.
- Everyone who lives in a brick house.
- Everyone who has been to New York.
- Everyone who plays on a soccer team.
- Everyone who has the number "4" in his or her address.
- Everyone who went to camp last summer.
- Everyone who likes to snowboard.
- Everyone who can quote a Bible verse.
- Everyone who has a dog.
- Everyone who is an only child.
- Everyone who has been on an airplane.
- Everyone who rode in a van today.
- Everyone who has carpet on his or her bedroom floor.
- Everyone who likes macaroni and cheese.

Take It Another Step

Informally give the children opportunity to ask YOU and the other teachers questions so they can become better acquainted with you.

Getting to Know You
Name Game

Goal: To encourage children to get to know each other's name. If your group is small and everyone knows each other well, your goal could be to see how quickly you can play this game.

What Do I Need?

- Balls or beanbags

How Do I Do It?

- Children stand in a circle.
- Give a child a ball and instruct him or her to throw or roll it to another child while saying his or her own name and the other person's name: "Andrew to Blake." Then Blake throws it to someone else: "Blake to Kayley." Encourage the children to move faster and faster, and then introduce another ball into the circle so two balls are going back and forth with children calling out names. Children cannot throw the ball to someone standing or sitting right next to them. If the circle is large and children are fairly coordinated, start with two balls. To add to the fun, add more balls. (Beanbags can be used instead of balls.)

Take It Another Step

See if the children know the names of all the teachers by having teachers play the game, too.

61

Getting to Know You
Your Name Is What?

Goal: To encourage children to get to know each other better.

What Do I Need?

- Bibles

How Do I Do It?

- Have an informal discussion with your class as to the meanings of their names. Even young children often know why their parents named them what they did. Ask children to volunteer their stories rather than going around the room so that you don't embarrass children who don't know about the meanings of their names.

Take It Another Step

Bring in a book on names and their meanings and help children find their names. You may also talk about the meanings of some of the familiar names in the Bible. (See below.)

Familiar Bible names and their meanings.

- Sarah—Princess   Genesis 17:15
- Samuel—Asked of God   1 Samuel 1:20
- Eve—Life-giving   Genesis 3:20
- Peter—Rock   Matthew 16:18
- Solomon—Peaceful   1 Kings 11:42

Getting to Know You
Hi, My Name Is Ty

Goal: To encourage children to get to know each other better.

What Do I Need?

- Paper and pencil for each child

How Do I Do It?

- Tell the children to write a two-line poem about themselves. The poem should give their names and information about them.
- Give them some ideas to get them started.

> I am Madison and I go to the mall.
> I also draw and kick soccer balls.
>
> I'm 11 years old and my name is Mark.
> Last summer our family went to Glacier Park.
>
> I love Jesus and Emma is my name.
> Last week I got to go to a Dodgers game.

- After giving the children time to write, allow them to read their poetry to each other.

If you have time, assemble all the poems together in a book and add several lines so that it becomes a class poem.

Take It Another Step

Encourage the children to add more lines to their poems or to illustrate their poems.

Getting to Know You
The Face Is Familiar

Goal: To encourage children to get to know each other better.

What Do I Need?

- Paper and crayons or markers for each child

How Do I Do It?

- Allow the children to space themselves around the room so that others can't see what they're drawing. The floor could be an option for a workspace.

- Tell each child to draw a picture that represents him or her. Draw a picture that represents you to help children get started. You may also give some ideas to help children get started: a soccer player might draw a picture of a soccer ball, an artist might draw paints and an easel, and a child from a large family might draw his or her brothers and sisters.
- Have the children hand the papers to you when they are finished. Tell them to keep them covered so others won't see.
- Mix the pictures up so they're in no particular order. Then show them to the class and allow children to guess which picture belongs to which person.

Take It Another Step

Let the children display their pictures on a bulletin board.

Introducing the Characters: Bible Men

Goal: For children to learn more about unfamiliar Bible characters.

What Do I Need?

- Bibles
- For each child—a copy of one of the following pages about men in the Bible (pp. 66-70)

How Do I Do It?

Choose one of the following ways:

- Divide class into small groups. Give each child a copy of the chosen page. Assign each group one or two characters. (The Bible doesn't give a lot of information about some of the characters.) The small group reads about the character and then introduces him to the class. A volunteer from the group can tell his story; group members work together to present a skit or pantomime the actions of the character for others to guess; make posters or make pages for a Who's Who in the Bible? book.

- For older children, give each child a copy of the chosen page. Assign each child a character, and allow time to read the information and/or Bible verses. Child then "becomes" that character and introduces himself to the class.

Take It Another Step

Have children find additional information about the people in a Bible dictionary or concordance.

Abijah (1 Samuel 8:1-10)

Oh my, this man was a troublemaker. He was the son of Samuel. (Samuel was a good guy who starting serving God when he was a little kid, remember?) Samuel chose Abijah and his brother, Joel, to be judges for Israel. But instead of being honest and following God like their father, these two men did bad stuff like accept bribes and other dishonest things.

This made the people angry. They told Samuel they needed a king, someone who could rule them well.

Samuel prayed to God about it.

God said that they weren't upset with Samuel; they were upset because they didn't want God as their king. God told Samuel to tell the people all the things that would happen if a human king was chosen. Samuel did exactly what God told him to do, but the people wouldn't listen.

And it all started with the dishonesty of Abijah and his brother, Joel.

Julius (Acts 27:1,3,43)

Julius was a centurion (a member of the Imperial Regiment) who was chosen to guard Paul and some other prisoners on their way to Rome. Even though he was a guard of the prisoners, he treated Paul with kindness. When they made a stop at Sidon, Julius allowed Paul to visit with friends so he could get cleaned up, rested and fed.

Later on in the journey, after a horrible storm shipwrecked the boat, some of the soldiers wanted to kill the prisoners so they wouldn't get away. Julius insisted that they NOT kill the prisoners and encouraged Paul and the others to jump overboard and swim to land. Paul's life was saved.

Joiada (Nehemiah 3:6)

Joiada was a good worker. He helped Nehemiah rebuild the walls of Jerusalem. In fact, we know exactly what he did. He laid the beams and put the doors, bolts and bars in place on the Jeshanah Gate.

Joram (2 Samuel 8:9-11)

Joram's dad was King Tou of Hamath. When David won the war with Hadedezer, Tou sent Joram to congratulate David with gifts of silver, gold and bronze. David, in turn, gave the gifts to the Lord as he did with what he gained from any battle.

Reuben (Genesis 37)

Sometimes Reuben was a good guy, but sometimes he was a bad guy. (Like all of us, right?)

Remember, Joseph's brothers didn't like Joseph because their father gave him a special coat. So when Jacob sent Joseph out to the field to see how his brothers were doing, it made for a bad scene. Joseph willingly went, but his brothers were not excited to see him.

In fact, when they saw him coming, they made a wicked plan. They would kill Joseph.

Reuben, the oldest brother, convinced his younger brothers to throw Joseph into a pit (old well) instead of killing him. Reuben tried to figure out how to rescue Joseph and take him back to Jacob. He walked off from his brothers for awhile (some Bible scholars think he was looking for help in rescuing his younger brother). But when he came back, he discovered that his younger brothers had sold Joseph to some traveling traders who were on their way to Egypt.

The good thing is that Reuben convinced his brothers NOT to kill Joseph. The bad thing is, as the older brother, he might have been able to talk them into NOT doing anything to Joseph.

Ahio (2 Samuel 6:3-6)

Ahio and his brother, Uzziah, were chosen to guide the Ark of the Covenant to Jerusalem. Important job, right? A new cart had been built and 30,000 men came to see the moving of the ark.

King David himself and a whole lot of musicians paraded in front of the cart as Ahio and Uzziah walked. The musicians played their instruments and sang praises. And everyone was happy—well, until one of the oxen tripped and Uzziah reached out to catch the ark.

Unfortunately, everyone had forgotten that God instructed that no one but the priests were to touch the ark.

David was afraid and he quickly had the ark put in the house of someone who lived nearby.

Gad (2 Samuel 24:11; 1 Chronicles 21:9-19; 1 Chronicles 29:29)

Gad was David's prophet and often told David what to do. When David disobeyed God and had his soldiers counted (instead of trusting God that his army was strong), Gad was the one who presented David with his punishment. Gad was also an author and musician. He wrote a book about David's life and helped with the worship music in the Temple.

Lucius (Acts 13:1-3)

Lucius was one of the church leaders in Antioch who appointed (ordained) Barnabas and Saul (Paul) to be missionaries. Do you know what it means for a pastor to be ordained? Usually today, a person must write down what he or she believes and answer a lot of questions from other pastors, professors or Bible scholars. If the people asking questions think the want-to-be-pastor knows enough about the Bible, they will ordain him or her. Teachers need their teacher certification. Lawyers need to pass the bar. Pastors need to be ordained.

Shem (Genesis 5:32)

This is kind of funny. Sometimes people think that Noah's sons were young men when they went onto the ark. Shem was born when Noah was 500 years old. Shem was 98 years old when he got on the ark. He was married, but he and his wife didn't have any kids until after the flood was over.

Gaddi (Numbers 13:11)

We know the names of the spies who chose to trust in God: Joshua and Caleb. Gaddi was from the tribe of Manasseh and was one of the spies who DIDN'T trust God to take the Israelites to the Promised Land.

Aaron (Exodus 32)

Aaron was the brother of Moses. When God spoke to Moses from the burning bush and told him he had been chosen to lead the Israelites out of Egypt, Moses panicked. Moses knew he wasn't a charming and eloquent speaker. How could he lead the Israelites? God told Moses to ask Aaron for help.

Later, when Moses was up on Mount Sinai talking with God about the Ten Commandments, Aaron was down with the people. Days went by and Moses did not come down. Those Israelites were always complaining about something and this time they complained that Moses was taking too long. They complained that Moses should've left them back in Egypt. They forgot the promises they had made to Moses and to God. They wanted action and they wanted it NOW! They complained to Aaron that they wanted a god to show them the way NOW!

Now, Aaron wasn't particularly brave. He was afraid of the people, so when they started complaining, he listened to them. He let them have a god. The people brought their gold jewelry to him and he melted it and formed it into a calf. He put it in the middle of the people and everyone was happy. They had a big celebration with a lot of food and then they bowed down before the calf and danced and sang. Obviously a calf couldn't hear them or lead them or answer their prayers or anything, but the people didn't pay any attention to that. God was angry with the people.

And Moses was angry with the people, too. He asked Aaron why he had let them do it and Aaron said he had thrown the gold in the fire and it came out a calf. Of course, THAT was a lie. Aaron had not been a good leader. He had allowed the people to disobey God.

Demetrius (Acts 19:24)

Demetrius made souvenirs in Ephesus. Unfortunately, they weren't good souvenirs. He made models of the temple of Artemis and maybe little "gods," too.

So when Paul came to town and started telling people about Christ and people started listening, the silver-temple business started doing poorly. Demetrius got the other silver-temple makers together to start a riot, but the town clerk settled it down long enough for Paul to get out of town.

Ezri (1 Chronicles 27:26)

Ezri was the head farmer during King David's reign. He made sure all the workers were doing their jobs.

Gaius (3 John)

Gaius would have been fun to know. He had a lot of money and was a VIP in his city. John wrote a letter to Gaius, praising him for being friendly to some strangers who had visited. Gaius' kindness was so fantastic, we can read about it even now, hundreds and hundreds of years later.

Mahlon (Ruth 1:2; 4:9-10; 5)

You think your name is weird! This son's parents named him "Mahlon" which means "sickly." How would you like to be called "sickly" for your whole, entire life? He was the son of Elimelech and Naomi and married Ruth. (Yes, the Ruth that the book is named after.) And he did die young because he was . . . umm . . . sickly.

Eutychus (Acts 20:7-12)

Talk about a long sermon! The Christians in the city of Troas were meeting together for a Bible study with Paul himself. Paul had a lot of things he wanted to tell the people because he was still talking at midnight.

Eutychus was there. He was a young man, sitting by an open window. Unfortunately, he was also tired and as Paul preached on, Eutychus got sleepier and sleepier until he finally drifted off to sleep and fell out the window—three stories up! Paul ran down to see what had happened. The men who reached him first declared him dead, but Paul said, "He is alive." Once again, Paul could not have done this miracle without God working through him. He did not have the power in himself to make the young man alive again, or even well enough to walk again.

Then, guess what happened?

Paul kept preaching until the sun rose.

Heman (1 Chronicles 15:16-22; 25:1-3)

Now, this was a family with its own band. Heman had 14 sons and 3 daughters and several brothers who were also musical. The Bible tells us that the Heman family sang and played the harp, lyre and cymbals for the Temple worship. Heman himself was skilled at playing the cymbals. Even some of the Psalms are thought to be authored by Heman or members of his family. (Can you find which Psalms?) How many people in your family sing or play an instrument?

Malachi (Malachi)

You know a book of the Bible is named after him, but how much more do you know? Not much, because no one does. Malachi was the last of the minor prophets and last of the Old Testament books. Bible scholars think that he lived during the time Nehemiah was rebuilding the wall of Jerusalem. Other than that, all we have is the message he wrote in his book.

Gaddi (Numbers 13:11)

We know the names of the spies who chose to trust in God: Joshua and Caleb. Gaddi was from the tribe of Manasseh and was one of the spies who DIDN'T trust God to take the Israelites to the Promised Land.

Simeon (Luke 2:25-35)

Simeon loved God and because he had the gift of prophecy, he knew that he would see the Messiah (Savior, Jesus) before he died. When Joseph and Mary brought the baby Jesus to the Temple, Simeon recognized the baby as the true Son of God, the One who was to bring salvation to the people. He held the baby Jesus in his arms and praised God. Joseph and Mary were surprised at Simeon's understanding of Jesus' identity and why Jesus came to earth.

Aquila (Acts 18)

Aquila made tents along with his wife, Priscilla. They were Jews so when the Roman emperor, Claudius, said that all Jews had to get out of town, they went to Corinth. That's where Aquila met the Apostle Paul and since Paul was also a tentmaker by trade, they became friends. When Paul later went to Ephesus to preach the gospel, Aquila and his wife went with him and even helped teach others. One man they helped was Apollos, a man from Alexandria, and later still, Apollos taught others. Another place in the Bible tells us that Aquila and Priscilla went back to Rome and the Christians met at their house. Aquila was a good man (with a good wife).

Caleb (Numbers 13)

Remember the 12 spies? Ten said "NO! We shouldn't go to that land of giants and great walled cities." Two said, "Yes, the people are big and the cities strong, but we should go! We can do it!" Caleb was one of those "let's go" people.

The people were so angry at Caleb and Joshua's "let's-go" report, that they wanted to stone them to death. (Nice people, right?)

But, because of Caleb's faithfulness, Caleb and Joshua would be the ONLY people over the age of 20 to enter the Promised Land. Think about it. That must have been difficult for Joshua and Caleb to say "yes," when the other 10 spies said "no."

Buzi (Ezekiel 1:3)

This is just one of those funny names. We know he was Ezekiel's father—that's all!

Onesimus (Philemon)

Onesimus had a BIG problem. He was the slave of Philemon and he did something wrong. We don't know exactly what he did, but many Bible scholars think he stole something. Rather than face his punishment, which could be as bad as death, Onesimus took off for Rome. There he met Paul and became a Christian. The letter of Philemon (a book of the Bible) is a personal look into the life of Paul, Philemon and Onesimus. You see, after he became a Christian, Onesimus was willing to go back to Philemon, but was afraid of what Philemon would do when he saw him. So Paul wrote a letter to Philemon explaining that Onesimus had trusted Christ and asking to give Onesimus another chance. Why not read Philemon and put yourself in the place of Paul or Onesimus or Philemon?

Xerxes (Esther 2:16)

Have you heard what happened to Esther? Well, Xerxes was her king. He is the one who selected Esther as queen. He is the one Esther went to with her plan to rescue the Jews. He is the one who listened to Esther and allowed for the "heads up" warning that the Jews would be attacked. Xerxes was a foolish and cruel man, but God worked through Esther and King Xerxes to save His people.

Introducing the Characters: Bible Women

Goal: For children to learn more about unfamiliar Bible characters.

What Do I Need?

- Bibles
- For each child—a copy of one of the following pages about women in the Bible (pp. 72-76)

How Do I Do It?

Choose one of the following ways:

- Divide class into small groups. Give each child a copy of the chosen page. Assign each group one or two characters. (The Bible doesn't give a lot of information about some of the characters.) The small group reads about the character and then introduces her to the class. A volunteer from the group can tell her story; group members can work together to present a skit or pantomime the actions of the character for others to guess; make posters or make pages for a "Who's Who in the Bible?" book.

- For older children, give each child a copy of the chosen page. Assign each child a character, and allow time to read the information and/or Bible verses. Child then "becomes" that character and introduces herself to the class.

Take It Another Step

When possible, have children find additional information about the people in a Bible dictionary or concordance.

Apphia (Philemon 2)

Apphia was a Christian lady who lived in Colosse. Some scholars think she might have been Philemon's wife (see Philemon 2). Or, if she was not his wife, she may have been a close relative, otherwise she would not have been mentioned at the beginning of Paul's letter to Philemon.

Bathsheba (1 Kings 1:11-31)

Bathsheba was the wife of David and the mother of Solomon, Shimea, Shobab and Nathan. Both Solomon and Nathan were ancestors of Christ. 1 Kings 1:11-31 tells how Bathsheba went to David as he lay dying and told him that his son Adonijah was celebrating his soon-to-be-kingship outside the city gates. (Adonijah's plan was not right.) David had promised that Solomon would be the next king so he had his servants get his own mule from his own stable and have Solomon ride though the city. All the servants were to shout "Long live King Solomon!" That's exactly what happened and Bathsheba's son, Solomon became king.

Nehushta (2 Kings 24:8)

Nehushta was the wife of King Jehoiakim and mother of Jehoiachin. Neither king followed God.

Huldah
(2 Chronicles 34:22-28)

Huldah was a prophetess in Jerusalem and keeper of the royal clothes. When King Josiah had the Temple cleaned, Shaphan (the secretary) found the Book of Law (the first five books of the Old Testament). The king sent Shaphan and some other men to inquire of the Lord what to do. They went to Huldah to get the answer.

Rhoda (Acts 12:13-16)

Remember when Peter's friends gathered together to pray for him because he was in prison? The prayer meeting was at the home of Mary (mother of John Mark). As they were praying, an angel visited Peter and led him out of the prison, past the guards and down the street. At first even Peter was confused about what was happening, but then he realized that God had sent an angel to free him.

When Peter figured out what was going on, he headed for John Mark's house and knocked on the door. Rhoda was the servant girl who went to the door and saw that Peter was standing there.

You can imagine how excited she was! They were praying that Peter would get out of prison and there he was RIGHT AT THE DOOR. In fact, she was SO excited, she forgot to open the door, but went back to where the people were praying and shouted, "Peter is at the door!"

Now wouldn't you think these people would be over-the-top excited to see Peter?

Well, instead of running to the door to see their friend (who had been left standing outside), they decided Rhoda was crazy!

Peter kept knocking, however, and FINALLY, they opened the door and saw their answer to prayer.

Introducing the Characters
Bible Women #2

Persis (Romans 16:12)

A Christian lady who lived in Rome and worked hard in serving the Lord.

Candace (Acts 8:27-40)

Candace is the name of the queen whose treasurer was visiting Jerusalem. (The name "Candace," however, probably did not refer to just one queen, but to an entire line of queens. Kind of like Pharaoh is the name of several kings.) But the treasurer of THIS Queen Candace was riding along in his chariot, reading the book of Isaiah. Philip saw the man and asked if he understood what he was reading. He didn't, so Philip helped him understand and the man trusted Christ as Savior.

Basemath (1 Kings 4:15)

This lady is worth mentioning just because of her name. How would YOU like to be called Basemath? Well, maybe if you liked math, it would be OK. Basemath was actually the daughter of Solomon. Just think, the wisest man in the world and he named his daughter Basemath. (Her name probably means "fragrant.")

Rahab (Joshua 2:1-21; 6:22-25; Matthew 1:5)

Rahab had not lived a very good life. But she had heard about the Israelites. She knew about the miracles of the Red Sea crossing and how with God on the side of the Israelites, they had defeated STRONG enemies. She also understood that God had promised Canaan to the Israelites. So when Joshua sent the spies to check out Jericho, she was willing to protect them by hiding them under the flax covering her roof. (Some Bible scholars think she might have made linen for a living.) When the city officials showed up at her door and demanded to see the spies, she sent them on a wild spy chase. As the officers set off to find them, she let them out of a window and made a deal. She had protected them, so they must protect her family when the Israelites fought Jericho. They agreed and DID protect the family during the battle.

Later Rahab married Salmon and they had a son named Boaz who had a son named Obed who had a son name Jesse who had a son named David. Yes, THAT David. This is the family line of Christ.

Jochebed (Numbers 26:59; Exodus 2:1-10)

Moses' mother. Jochebed is the smart mom who made the waterproof basket for her son and then hid him in the Nile River. Later, Pharaoh's daughter found him and Moses was raised a prince.

73

Elizabeth (Luke 1:5-22,57-64)

Elizabeth and Mary (the mother of Jesus) were cousins. Elizabeth was married to Zacharias, a priest at the Temple. They were good people, but were sad because they had no children. One day, while Zacharias was in the Temple, an angel came and told him that he they would have a child. OK, Zacharias was rather old, and thinking about becoming a father was rather surprising. So, he asked God for a sign and he immediately lost his speech. Elizabeth DID have a baby as God had promised and she named him John. Back then family names were big, and no one could figure out why she had named him John since no one else in the family had been named John. Zacharias wrote on a tablet (remember he couldn't talk), "His name is John." At that point he once again got his speech back. John, the son of Zacharias and Elizabeth was the man who told the good news that the Savior was coming!

Luke wrote about Zacharias and Elizabeth: "Both of them were upright in the sight of God, observing all the Lord's commandments and regulations blamelessly" (Luke 1:6). Wouldn't you like someone to say THAT about you?

Jemimah (Job 42:14)

Remember all those BIG problems Job had? Well, finally things started going well again and he had seven sons and three daughters. The daughters were Jemimah, Keziah and Keren-Happuch. The Bible tells us that they were the three most beautiful young ladies in all the land.

Phoebe (Romans 16:1-2)

A Christian lady who served in the church at Cenchrea. Bible scholars (smart people who study Bible words) think that she was wealthy and maybe a businesswoman who traveled. Some think she is the person who delivered Paul's letter to the Romans.

Noah (Numbers 27:1-11)

Yes, there's a girl Noah in the Bible. Nobody pays much attention to her because of the other Noah and his ark. Noah (the girl) and her sisters: Mahlah, Hoglah, Milcah and Tirzah (the daughters of Zelophehad) went before Moses with a special request. Their dad had died and he hadn't left any sons and therefore, the family name was about to disappear. They asked for a special inheritance. Moses went to the Lord and guess what? The Lord said, "The girls are right. Give them some land." Noah and her sisters were smart to go to Moses. Don't you think it would have been fun to *know a Noah?* (Ha! Ha!)

Puah (Exodus 1:15-22)

Puah was a good lady and a very brave one. She was a nurse who helped deliver the babies during the time of Pharaoh's decree that all baby boys should be killed. She and Shiphrah refused to do it and they let the babies live.

Bible Women #4

Damaris (Acts 17:32-34)

When the people mocked Paul because he was preaching the truth, Damaris listened. She understood that Paul knew what he was talking about and wanted to follow God. Damaris lived in Athens. Some people think she might have held some kind of high position in the city because her name is mentioned with a judge.

Noadiah (Nehemiah 6:14)

This lady was a real problem! She was a prophetess who tried to scare Nehemiah into NOT rebuilding the walls of Jerusalem. She was not a good person.

Joanna (Luke 24:10)

We don't know much about her, but we do know she was Chuza's wife. (Chuza was the man who took care of Herod Agrippa's house.) The most special thing about Joanna, however, is that she was one of the ladies who came to the tomb after Jesus died to put spices on his grave and therefore, saw Jesus after He came alive again.

Tabitha (Acts 9:36-41)

Tabitha, who had the Greek name Dorcas, was a good friend to the people around her. She made clothes for the poor and people liked her. But one day she became sick and died. Her friends were sad. When they heard that one of the disciples, Peter, was nearby in a town called Lydda, they sent two men to ask him to come right away!

Peter agreed. Tabitha's friends took him upstairs to her room and showed him ALL the CLOTHES she had made. Can't you just imagine them crying and talking over one another? "Peter, look at all the good she has done!" "Peter, look at this half-finished robe. She was making it for the poor widow down the road." "Peter, she was such a sweet lady, she can't die."

Peter sent them out of the room, got down on his knees and prayed. Then he said, "Tabitha, get up." Amazing! She opened her eyes and sat up! (Of course, God was the one who caused Tabitha to come back to life. Peter couldn't have done it on his own.)

Then Peter called all her friends and presented her to them. (Can you imagine their conversation THEN?) People all over Joppa heard about what happened and believed on the Lord.

Eunice (Acts 16:1; 2 Timothy 1:5)

Even though Eunice is only mentioned in two verses, she is an example of a good mom. Remember Timothy? The young man who learned to love and obey Jesus at an early age? The Apostle Paul told Timothy about God and Timothy trusted Christ as His Savior. Timothy then went on to help Paul and his ministry and to become a young pastor, himself. Two of Paul's letters (books of the Bible) are written to Timothy. (Can you guess which ones they are?) Eunice was Timothy's mom and she is praised for teaching Timothy the Scripture from the time he was a young boy. What are you learning now? Maybe someday you will be a pastor or missionary like Timothy.

Introducing the Characters
Bible Women #5

Deborah
(Judges 4:4-24; Judges 5)

This is ANOTHER Deborah. This Deborah was a judge and prophetess (someone who tells a message about God). She sat under "the palm tree of Deborah" and people came to her and told her their problems. She helped them solve their arguments.

She sent a message to Barak and told him that God wanted him to fight against Sisera, the king of Canaan. Sisera was a mean guy. His big goal in life was to terrorize Israel, and he had been doing it for 20 years.

Now, Barak said he'd go if Deborah went with him. So Deborah agreed and off they went to fight Sisera. They had 10,000 men in their army and Sisera had multitudes of men, plus 900 iron chariots. But God was on the side of Israel and Israel won.

After Israel won the battle, Barak and Deborah sang a song of praise to God for the victory. What would you sing after a battle? You can read the words of Barak and Deborah's song in Judges 5. That's kind of cool that we can read it because some people say it is one of the earliest examples of Hebrew poetry. (So, you're not ALL that interested in Hebrew poetry—still think about it. These words were sung hundreds and hundreds of years ago and we can read them!)

Deborah (Genesis 24:50; 35:8)

We don't read much about this Deborah in the Bible, but she must have been a kind and faithful lady. She was Rebekah's nurse (that means she took care of Rebekah when Rebekah was growing up). When Rebekah went back to Mesopotamia to become Isaac's bride, Deborah went with her. There she took care of Rebekah's twins, Jacob and Esau. When she died, she was buried under an oak tree that was named "oak of weeping" in memory of such a good, faithful and caring person.

Orpah (Ruth 1:4)

Orpah was the daughter-in-law of Naomi, wife of Naomi's son, Mahlon. When Naomi decided to leave Moab and go back to Bethlehem, Orpah chose to stay in Moab while Ruth went with Naomi.

Taphath (1 Kings 4:11)

Taphath was a daughter of King Solomon. She married Solomon's supply officer.

Euodia and Syntyche
(Philippians 4:2-3)

Unfortunately, these women caused a BIG problem. They attended the church in Philippi and everything about that church seemed to be going well. Paul commended the church on their teaching, their attitude and their service. Because the church was doing well, many people were trusting Christ as their Savior.

Only these two ladies were making trouble. They had argued with each other and wouldn't let it go. The argument was so bad, that Paul heard about it way back in Rome. Now, in his letter to the church, he begs them to make it right and work together again. He even asks other people in the church to help them. He tells them, "Rejoice!" Rejoicing seems to be the last thing on their minds.

Even today there are people who argue with each other and cause trouble all round!

Laughing at a Riddle

Goal: To smile, and learn more about the Bible. Some of these are corny and have been around for awhile, but use them to catch the interest of children. Then take advantage of the discussion and teach a little about the circumstances surrounding the Bible character or event. (Remind the children that even though some of the riddles make us laugh, many of these events were very serious and sad.)

What Do I Need?

- Bibles
- List of riddles (choose from pp. 78-80)

How Do I Do It?

- Ask the riddles and give children an opportunity to guess the answer.
- Review the background of the character or event.

Take It Another Step

You may wish to begin or end your class with a riddle each week. Challenge children to make up their own riddles.

Laughing at a Riddle
Bible Riddles #1

1. Question: What Bible woman was extra smart about finances?

Answer: Pharaoh's daughter. She went to the bank of the Nile River and received a good profit (prophet).

Exodus 2:1-9—Pharaoh's daughter discovered Moses floating in the basket in the Nile River. She raised him as her own. Later God used Moses to bring the Israelite people out of Egypt.

2. Question: When was baseball first mentioned in the Bible?

Answer: Genesis 1:1—"In the big inning . . . ."

Genesis 1:1 talks about the beginning of the world as we know it—the beginning of God's creation of the heaven and the earth.

3. Question: What happened in that "big inning?"

Answer: Eve stole first, Adam stole second, Cain struck out Abel, and the Prodigal Son came home.

Genesis 3:6—Eve took the fruit and gave some to Adam.
Genesis 4:8—Cain killed Abel.
Luke 25:11-32—The story of the son who took his inheritance and went away from home. He spent it all in partying until he was left feeding pigs for a living. He understood that his father's servants were living better than he was, so he decided to go home and beg forgiveness. But his father loved him so much, he welcomed him home with a big celebration.

4. Question: Who was the funniest man in the Bible?

Answer: Samson because he brought the house down—a phrase that means to make people laugh.

Judges 16—Samson was the strongest man in the Bible, but listened to the smooth-talking Delilah and gave away the secret of his strength which was his hair. The Philistines were overjoyed. They cut Samson's hair, blinded him and bound him with bronze shackles. They took him to the temple of their false God and told him to entertain the people. Samson asked to be put between two pillars and asked God to give him back his strength just one more time. God did so, and Samson was able to knock down the temple by his strength.

5. Question: Who was a good babysitter?

Answer: David, he rocked Goliath to sleep.

1 Samuel 17—David was not part of the Israelite army, but was on the battlefield to bring food to his older brothers. But he rose to the challenge of fighting Goliath and with his shepherd's slingshot and a small stone downed the giant. God used David to help win the battle with the Philistines.

Laughing at a Riddle
Bible Riddles #2

1. Question: Who was the best mathematician in the Bible?

   Answer: Moses, because he wrote the book of Numbers.

Moses wrote the first five books of the Bible: Genesis, Exodus, Leviticus, Numbers, Deuteronomy. These first five books are sometimes called "The Torah," "The Law" or "Pentateuch." Would you like to learn some Greek? Pentateuch is the Greek word for five volumes. The first five books of the Bible are a five-volume set of books written by Moses.

2. Question: Who was the shortest man in the Bible?

   Answer: Bildad the Shuhite (shoe height).

Job 2:11—Bildad was one of Job's friends. Remember just about everything Job had was taken away from him. Three friends decided to give him comfort. However, with friends like these, Job needed NO enemies.

3. Question: Why did Job end up in bed with a cold?

   Answer: He had poor comforters. (His friends tried to comfort him, but didn't.)

Job—This is another riddle about Job's three friends. They tried to comfort him, but they did a horrible job!

4. Question: How do we know Abraham was a smart man?

   Answer: He knew a Lot.

Genesis 12:4—Lot was Abraham's nephew. When Abraham left his home and moved to Canaan, Lot went with him. Later Abraham gave Lot his choice of the land and Lot chose the best land for himself.

5. Question: Where is Solomon's Temple?

   Answer: On the side of his head.

1 Kings 6-7—One of the greatest events of Solomon's reign was the building of the Temple. Can you believe it took him seven years to do it? That's because Solomon wanted everything "just right," elegant, and beautiful. More than 100,000 men worked on just the lumber-and-stone-cutting part of the project! That was some Temple.

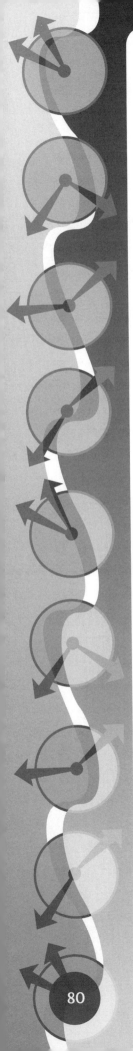

Laughing at a Riddle
Bible Riddles #3

1. **Question:** Why couldn't Noah's family fish while on the ark?

   Answer: They only had two worms.

2. **Question:** How did Noah light the ark?

   Answer: He used floodlights.

3. **Question:** What did Noah say when he walked off the ark?

   Answer: "I should have killed those mosquitos when I had the chance!"

4. **Question:** Did you hear about Noah's canning factory?

   Answer: He had a boat full of preserved pairs.

5. **Question:** Where did Noah keep the bees?

   Answer: In the ark-hives (archives).

6. **Question:** What animal took the most luggage on the ark? Which animal took the least?

   Answer: The elephant took the most—his trunk. The rooster only brought his comb.

7. **Question:** Where was Noah when the lights went off?

   Answer: In d'ark.

8. **Question:** What did the one cat say to the other cat as they left the ark?

   Answer: "Is that AraRAT?"

9. **Question:** How do we know that Noah was the fourth person out of the ark?

   Answer: Because the Bible says that Noah went forth (Genesis 8:18, *KJV*).

Learning About Missions

Where's the Country?

Goal: To have fun and learn about the missionaries your church or denomination supports.

What Do I Need?

- A world map or globe
- Information (prayer cards, newsletters, etc.) about missionaries your church or denomination supports
- Wrapped bite-size pieces of candy or small prizes

How Do I Do It?

- Have children sit on the floor in front of the world map or globe.
- Name a missionary your church or denomination supports and the country where that missionary serves. The first child to raise a hand goes to the map and points out the country. (Note: If children have difficulty locating countries, play Hot or Cold. Child puts finger on map or globe and moves finger depending on your directions ("warmer" or "hot" means moving closer to the country, "colder" or "freezing" means moving away from the country).

- Give a piece of candy or some other small prize when a child finds the country.
- Continue as time and interest permit. Limit a child to finding one country until everyone who wishes to has had an opportunity to participate. (In games like this, you'll probably find children who have studied world maps and can find any country. Other children may have little idea of country locations. Be ready to give clues as needed.)

Take It Another Step

Combine this activity with the missionary letter or e-mail suggested in the "Writing a Letter" section.

Learning About Missions
Designing a Missionary Book

Goal: To have fun and learn about the missionaries your church or denomination supports. (This activity could be an on-going project, collecting information piece by piece over several weeks or even months as you encounter those spare minutes.)

What Do I Need?

- A copy of Missions Discovery (p. 84) for each child
- Information (prayer cards, newsletters, etc.) about missionaries your church or denomination supports
- 8½x11-inch (21.5x28-cm) white paper and construction paper
- Thin-tip markers
- Pens
- Three-ring binder
- Plastic-page protectors

How Do I Do It?

- Assign or let each child choose a missionary. If your class is large, divide into groups (with an adult). Assign each group one missionary. (If your church supports more than a dozen missionaries, choose the ones with whom your children are already familiar so that the children will be better able to connect faces with a places.)
- Give each child or group the missionary information you have collected and a copy of the Missions Discovery page. Children answer as many questions on the page as they can.
- Each child creates a page for his or her assigned missionary by writing or drawing information about the missionary on a sheet of construction paper or white paper.
- Children insert completed pages into plastic-page protectors and place into binder.

Take It Another Step

- Assign individual children to complete the information on a particular country as bonus work to do at home.
- Ask the children to list additional questions they would ask a missionary.
- The next time one of the missionaries visits your church, invite him or her to speak to your group and answer the questions.

Optional Ideas

- Instead of collecting information about a variety of missionaries, focus on just one missionary. (If possible, choose one who is scheduled to be at your church in the near future.)
- Instead of putting the information in a notebook, children work together to create a large poster. Write a title across the top of the a sheet of poster board such as: "Introducing You to _____" Hang the completed poster in your classroom or on a missionary bulletin board in your church. When the missionary visits the church, the children will have an instant connection.
- If you make a poster, get permission to hang it in a prominent place in a church hallway, so that everyone can learn a little about the missionary.
- Children may also do on-the-spot research, if you have a classroom computer with Internet access. Here are some guidelines: First, make sure your church has restrictive filters in place. (You might be there guiding the search during class, but children can come back later when no adults are present. Remember, children are often more computer savvy than adults, so protect yourself, the child and the church by limiting access. You may also choose to print out Internet pages before class.)

Second, several missionary organizations (such as Wycliffe, North American Mission Board, etc.) have a children's page that provide information on different countries and cultures. Others (Greater Europe Mission is one example) have country spotlights or profiles, so information about a specific country can be obtained safely without searching several unknown sites.

Third, if you're looking for information about a country and don't know which websites will provide that information, tourism sites are a good place to start. Put in keywords such as "Kenya tourism" or "Israel tourism." Tourism sites are usually child safe and often offer beautiful pictures of the country's cities, scenic spots or animals.

Missions Discovery

Country Questions

1. What is the capital of the country where the missionary serves?

2. What is the climate like?

3. What kind of food is eaten in this country?

4. What kind of animals live in the country?

5. What do the people do for a living?

Personal Questions

1. Where does the missionary live?

2. What does the missionary do to help others learn about Jesus?

3. Is the missionary married? Children?

4. How long has the missionary served in the country?

Learning About Missions
Praying for the Missionaries

Goal: To pray for the missionaries whom your church or denomination supports.

What Do I Need?

- Information (prayer cards, newsletters, etc.) about missionaries your church or denomination supports
- Whiteboard or large sheet of paper and markers

How Do I Do It?

- Ask the children to look at the missionary information, and then lead them to brainstorm different prayer topics (see below) and related requests. List topics and requests on a whiteboard or paper. (Since you are using this as an instant activity, you probably don't know immediate needs.)

Some General Topics:

- Pray for the country's overall political situation.
- Thank the Lord for government officials who are allowing missionaries to serve.
- Pray for people in the country who believe in false gods. (Tell children about the predominant religions of the country.)
- Pray for the country's Christians that they may have the courage they need to love and obey God.
- Pray for new Christians who may be experiencing family conflict because the family rejects Christianity. (Explain to the children that in some countries, people who trust the Lord Jesus Christ as Savior are out of favor with their families and sometimes are even told to leave their homes.)
- Pray for churches and ministries in the country that are reaching out to those people who don't know Christ.

Some Personal Topics:

- Pray for the missionary family that they will have wisdom in serving God.
- Pray that the missionaries will be good team members in getting a project done well.
- Pray that new missionaries will quickly learn the language so they can communicate.
- Pray that the missionary will relate well to the people who live in the country.
- Pray that the missionary will find friends in the country.
- Pray that the missionary family will not be lonely.
- Thank the Lord that the missionary is willing to work in that country.
- Pray that the missionary will show kindness and wisdom in working with the people and teaching them about the Bible.
- Pray by name for the children in the missionary family.

Take It Another Step

If your church has a supply of missionary prayer cards, hand out one card to each child and encourage that child to place the card on a dresser, mirror, etc. and pray for the missionary each day.

85

Learning About Missions
Figuring Out the Cities

Goal: To help children understand that many missionaries work in cities (sometimes children think all missionaries work in remote areas with no modern conveniences).

What Do I Need?

- A copy of the Match the City game (p. 87) for each child
- Match the City Answer Key (p. 88)
- A pencil for each child
- A world map or globe

Learning About Missions
Match the City

When your teacher tells you "GO," match up the cities and countries by drawing a line between the two.

EGYPT	VIENNA
KENYA	BERLIN
ETHIOPIA	KABUL
SOUTH AFRICA	ATHENS
AFGHANISTAN	CAPE TOWN
CHINA	MOSCOW
INDIA	BANGKOK
UNITED KINGDOM	DUBLIN
ISRAEL	OTTAWA
JAPAN	ADDIS ABABA
THAILAND	PARIS
AUSTRIA	LONDON
FRANCE	CAIRO
GERMANY	NAIROBI
GREECE	BEIJING
UNITED STATES	TOKYO
IRELAND	NEW DELHI
IRAQ	NEW YORK CITY
RUSSIA	BAGHDAD
CANADA	JERUSALEM

© 2008 Gospel Light. Permission to photocopy granted in original purchase only. *The Big Book of Time Fillers*

How Do I Do It?

- Give each child a copy of Match the City game. Allow children five minutes or so to match the city with the country. (If you have younger and older children, form groups that include a mix of ages and allow them to work together on the game. Be prepared for some children to know a lot about other countries and for some children to know little.)
- Review the answers together. If time permits, look at a world map or globe and allow the children to find the countries they missed and fill in the answers.

Take It Another Step

On a large sheet of paper, make four columns with these titles: "Missionaries who live and work in big cities"; "Missionaries who live and work in small towns"; "Missionaries who travel a lot"; "Missionaries who live and work in remote areas." Look at a list of missionaries supported by your church or denomination and write their names in the appropriate column. Display in your classroom. (During the week, check with a church staff member or missions' team member about missionaries with whom you're unfamiliar. Report what you find to the class the following week.)

Learning About Missions
Match the City

When your teacher tells you "GO," match up the cities and countries by drawing a line between the two.

EGYPT	VIENNA
KENYA	BERLIN
ETHIOPIA	KABUL
SOUTH AFRICA	ATHENS
AFGHANISTAN	CAPE TOWN
CHINA	MOSCOW
INDIA	BANGKOK
UNITED KINGDOM	DUBLIN
ISRAEL	OTTAWA
JAPAN	ADDIS ABABA
THAILAND	PARIS
AUSTRIA	LONDON
FRANCE	CAIRO
GERMANY	NAIROBI
GREECE	BEIJING
UNITED STATES	TOKYO
IRELAND	NEW DELHI
IRAQ	NEW YORK CITY
RUSSIA	BAGHDAD
CANADA	JERUSALEM

Match the City Answer Key

When your teacher tells you "GO," match up the cities and countries by drawing a line between the two.

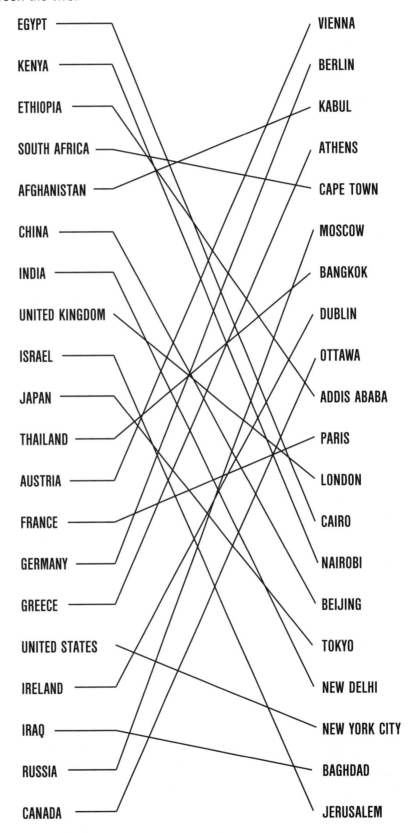

EGYPT	VIENNA
KENYA	BERLIN
ETHIOPIA	KABUL
SOUTH AFRICA	ATHENS
AFGHANISTAN	CAPE TOWN
CHINA	MOSCOW
INDIA	BANGKOK
UNITED KINGDOM	DUBLIN
ISRAEL	OTTAWA
JAPAN	ADDIS ABABA
THAILAND	PARIS
AUSTRIA	LONDON
FRANCE	CAIRO
GERMANY	NAIROBI
GREECE	BEIJING
UNITED STATES	TOKYO
IRELAND	NEW DELHI
IRAQ	NEW YORK CITY
RUSSIA	BAGHDAD
CANADA	JERUSALEM

Learning About Missions
In Any Language

Goal: To show children that the Bible is the same in any language.

What Do I Need?

- John 3:16 in another language (see p. 90)
- Whiteboard or paper and marker

How Do I Do It?

- Write out the verse and tell children this is John 3:16 in (language).
- Optional: If there is a teacher or child in your group who speaks another language, ask him or her to teach the verse to the group.
- Remind the children that even though you can write and say John 3:16 in many different languages, the message is the same: God loves us so much, He sent His Son to die for our sin. People choose to become missionaries so that they can help others learn the message of John 3:16.

Take It Another Step

Some children may have relatives who are fluent in another language. Ask them to ask their parents, grandparents, etc. to write down John 3:16 in that language. See how many different languages you can collect. Display them on a bulletin board.

John 3:16 Translations

Here is John 3:16 in four other languages.

French

Car Dieu a tant aimé le monde, qu'il a donné son Fils unique, afin que quiconque croit en Lui ne périsse point, mais qu'il ait la vie éternelle. (John 3:16)

German

Denn so hat Gott die Welt geliebt, daß er seinen eingeborenen Sohn gab, damit jeder, der an ihn glaubt, nicht verloren gehe, sondern ewiges Leben habe. (John 3:16)

Swahili

Kwa maana Mungu aliupenda ulimwengu kiasi cha kumtoa Mwanae pekee, ili kila mtu amwaminiye asipotee, bali awe na uzima wa milele. (John 3:16)

Spanish

Porque tanto amó Dios al mundo, que dio a su Hijo unigénito, para que todo el que cree en él no se pierda, sino que tenga vida eterna. (John 3:16).

Learning About Missions

Countries and Jobs

Goal: To show children in a fun way the variety of countries in which a missionary can serve and the variety of jobs which a missionary can do.

What Do I Need?

- A ball, beanbag or other object you can throw. (An excellent "ball" choice for this activity would be an inflatable globe. They are inexpensive and can be purchased at toy stores or teacher supply stores.)

How Do I Do It?

- Tell the children to stand in a circle.
- Give the first child the ball. Child says the name of a country and then tosses it to another child. Continue until most commonly-known countries have been named. Then change the challenge to: Name a job a missionary might do. (Note: As game is being played, stop the game when needed to explain anything you think some children may not understand. "Botswana is in Africa" or "Sure, electricians are needed in other countries. Electricians install and repair equipment in Bible schools, hospitals and churches.")
- If children quickly get stuck on countries or jobs, challenge the teachers to call out the places or jobs before a child throws the ball. Children will still be learning how many different places in which a missionary may live and the variety of jobs a missionary can do. For a list of 20 countries see the Match the City game (p. 87).

Jobs may include: pastor, teacher, church planter, Bible school professor, mechanic, pilot, musician, carpenter, doctor, nurse, artist, writer, principal, maintenance person, child-care giver, radio technician, computer technician, radio speaker, administrator, etc.

- Optional: Throw the ball to a child and invite that child to pray for the people in a particular country. Keep the prayer time meaningful. If children get too distracted with the ball throwing, simply throw throw the ball and assign countries. Once each child has been assigned a country, have children sit down. Have children pray.

Take It Another Step

Ask children to write down two careers they would like to do as an adult. Talk about ways these careers could be used to serve others in a foreign country.

Learning About Missions
I Hear Music

Goal: To teach children about different cultures in a unique way.

What Do I Need?

- A CD of children's music from one or more countries
- A CD player
- A ball, beanbag or other object you can throw. (An excellent "ball" choice for this activity would be an inflatable globe.)

How Do I Do It?

- Play an active, fun game while children listen to music from other countries. Children sit or stand in a circle.
- As you play the music CD, children pass the object around the circle. Stop the music after 10 to 15 seconds. As soon as the music stops, children stop passing the object. Child who is holding the object names a country in the world. Continue playing game, with children naming different countries each round.

Take It Another Step

Play the music (without playing the game) and see if children can guess the instruments.

Learning About Missions
Going on a Trip

Goal: To challenge children to think about a missionary's life. (This is a good activity for older children.)

What Do I Need?
- Chairs set up in rows to represent the inside of a plane
- Paper rectangles to represent boarding passes

How Do I Do It?
- Choose a country you would like to focus on—perhaps one where a church missionary serves. Tell the children they are taking a pretend mission trip to another country.
- Tell the children they will be gone for three years and lead them to brainstorm items they will need to bring. Encourage items for both ministry needs and personal needs. For example, ministry needs might be: Bible, books, paper, markers, computer, etc. Personal needs would include: clothes, medicine, books to read, games, etc

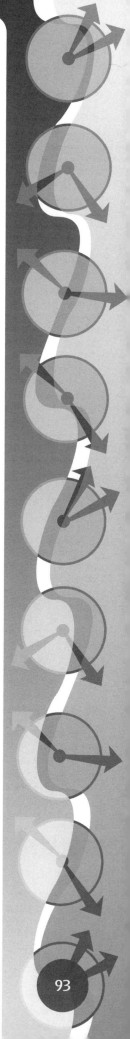

- Explain to the children that some missionaries live in countries with a lot of stores. Other missionaries live in countries that don't have certain products. Some countries have a lot of good food available, but might not have that one particular candy bar a missionary enjoys.
- Children line up to board airplane. Pretend as if you're ready to take their boarding passes, and then stop and say something like, "Wait, do you have your passport? Do you have your visa? Have you had your medical exam? Do you have your shots?" (The purpose of these questions is to let the children know there is a lot of preparation missionaries complete before getting on the plane.)
- After checking their "papers," allow children to get on the plane. Tell them they'll be on the plane for 12 hours, so they might as well relax.
- Lead children to brainstorm what they'll have to do when they get off the plane. Encourage them to give answers such as: find a place to live, find a place to buy food, learn the language, get to know the people, etc.
- Periodically, make comments that will teach children something about the country ("We'll find it hot when we get off the plane because the average temperature here is in the eighties." Or, "We'll see a large city with skyscrapers. That's Tokyo the capital of Japan.")

Take It Another Step

Choose a particular country for the year. Whenever you have some time to fill, "travel" to that country and teach the children something else about the culture. By the end of the year, they will know a lot of facts.

Learning About Missions
A Mission Object Talk

Goal: To teach an object lesson that helps children learn about the importance of missions.

What Do I Need?

- Play dough

How Do I Do It?

- Hand out a fist-sized lump of play dough to each child. Children form shapes of their own choosing. After giving them a few minutes, stop them. Take any objects or figures they have made and line them up on a table.
- Teach the following lesson.

These figures look so beautiful. (Child's name), I especially like that snake (dog, cat, hamburger, cupcake) that you made. I think that should be an idol. "Snake, please crawl off the table!" (Pause as if waiting for the snake to follow your instructions.) Hmmm . . . that's funny—the snake isn't moving.

Oh, I know what's wrong. I'm not the one who made the snake. (Child's name), you tell the snake to do something. (Look puzzled as you wait for the snake to obey the child's command.)

What's wrong here, anyhow? (Some child will probably tell you that the snake isn't alive.)

That's true, and of course we know that objects we've made from play dough aren't really alive and can't help us. But think back to Aaron and the golden calf (see Exodus 32). Who can tell me what happened when Moses was on the mountain talking to God? (Allow children to relate the details. Supplement as needed.) Was throwing a bunch of gold into a fire and making a calf to worship any more intelligent than trying to get these play dough figures to do something?

No. Neither one of them worked because the finished idol wasn't alive.

All over the world, people are making gods out of rock and metal and precious stones. They don't seem to understand that something that isn't alive can't help them.

John wrote a simple verse that we need to remember. 1 John 5:21 says "Dear children, keep yourselves from idols."

Another verse in the Bible says: "For even if there are so-called gods, whether in heaven or on earth (as indeed there are many "gods" and many "lords"), yet for us there is but one God, the Father, from whom all things came and for whom we live; and there is but one Lord, Jesus Christ, through whom all things came and through whom we live. But not everyone knows this" (1 Corinthians 8:5-7).

That's why missionaries need to go to other countries. That's why we need to tell people that there is only one God and He is alive! He's not made out of play dough, rock, metal or precious stones. He is living!

Missionaries tell the good news that our God is the true God. We can do that, too, right here in our own town. When we are friendly to visitors to our church, to our neighbors and to others at school, it's a wonderful way to share God's love with others.

Take It Another Step

From the Internet, print out some pictures of idols that people worship today and show them to your children.

Learning About Missions

A Game to Play

Goal: To play a fun game while thinking about the many places a person can be a missionary and the many things that a missionary needs.

What Do I Need?

- No supplies needed for this activity

How Do I Do It?

- Tell the children to sit in a circle. The first child says: "I am traveling to _____ (name of a place that starts with *A*) to be a missionary." The second child says the sentence, repeats the first child's destination and adds a destination that starts with *B*. The third child continues, adding a third destination that starts with *C*.

- If a child misses, he or she drops out of the game. When two children are out of the game, start a new round.
- After several rounds, vary the game. This time the first child says: "I am leaving on a missionary trip and I am taking my _____ (something that starts with *A* such as "apple juice"). Game continues as before with each child adding items that begin with succeeding letters of the alphabet (Bible, comb, dog, etc.).

Take It Another Step

If you have an older group of children, challenge then to play a more difficult version of this game by saying the country and the purpose for the visit (to teach school, to build wells, to work in a hospital, etc.) in one turn.

Learning About Missions
A Book to Read

Goal: To introduce children to a missionary.

What Do I Need?

- An exciting children's missionary biography

How Do I Do It?

- Read a few children's missionary biographies and choose one to read to your class. Look for good writing, an adventurous story and biblical soundness. (Note: There are also some good missionary DVDs available. Although they are longer than an "instant activity," they are a good resource for your classroom.)
- Keep the chosen biography in a handy place in your classroom.
- When time allows, read a chapter or two aloud to children. (If needed, briefly summarize previous chapters before reading a new chapter.)

Take It Another Step

Work with your church librarian to make a list of missionary biographies for the children in your class. Encourage the children to take advantage of the library and read the books. Invite a child who reads one of the books to give a brief report as an instant activity.

Learning About Missions
How Can I Serve?

Goal: To teach children that they can serve the Lord.

What Do I Need?

- Bibles

How Do I Do It?

- Tell children that today they are going to find some ways that they can serve the Lord. Have the children find the Bible verses listed below. Ask a volunteer to read the verse aloud. Ask the reader to tell what the main idea of the verse is. Allow other children to help with the explanation. Discuss each verse using the suggested conversation.

1. We Can Pray

Colossians 4:3—"And pray for us, too, that God may open a door for our message, so that we may proclaim the mystery of Christ, for which I am in chains."

Imagine! Paul was writing to the people of Colosse while he was in prison, yet he still wanted people to pray that he would have the opportunity to talk about Christ. When might kids your age have opportunities to talk about Jesus?

2. Study and Learn About God's Word So You Can Help Others

1 Peter 3:15—"But in your hearts set apart Christ as Lord. Always be prepared to give an answer to everyone who asks you to give the reason for the hope that you have. But do this with gentleness and respect."

Learn as much as you can about the Bible. Then, when you have the opportunity to tell a friend about Christ, you can answer the questions your friend might have. (But remember, no one has all the answers. If someone asks you something and you don't know the answer, tell the person you'll check with your pastor, children's pastor, Sunday School teacher, etc. Then get back to your friend with the answer.) What's something you already know about the Bible or Jesus that you think is important for others to know?

3. Work Together as a Team

1 Corinthians 12:19-22—"If they were all one part, where would the body be? As it is, there are many parts, but one body. The eye cannot say to the hand, 'I don't need you!' And the head cannot say to the feet, 'I don't need you!' On the contrary, those parts of the body that seem to be weaker are indispensable."

We are all different parts of one body and we can work together to get the job done. What is an example of a time people at church can work together to get something done that helps people learn about Jesus? (In the Christmas program, one child gets the lead part. Another child gets to work on the sets. Another child gets to hand out the programs as people arrive. All the jobs are important!)

4. Help Those in Need

Hebrews 13:16—"And do not forget to do good and to share with others, for with such sacrifices God is pleased."

That doesn't mean just giving a few cans of food to a food drive. This verse means also taking the time during recess to kick a soccer ball with the kid who is still learning how to play the game. What's another way kids your age can obey this verse?

5. Be an Example in the Way You Act

1 Timothy 4:12—"Don't let anyone look down on you because you are young, but set an example for the believers in speech, in life, in love, in faith and in purity."

You might be young, but you can still share God's love in the way you talk, the way you live and the way you love.

Here is a true story: A man taught science in a public high school. He knew nothing about the Lord, although he did have a Christian friend who told the teacher about Christ. The teacher didn't want to listen. He didn't care and he didn't see that believing the Bible made any difference in a person's life. But then he noticed something. Every year there were kids in his class who were kinder, friendlier and better workers than the other kids. All these kinder-friendlier-hard-working kids were from the same church—a church that believed the Bible. That made him wonder, *Why were Christians different?* He told his friend he would go to church with him. After hearing the message, the teacher trusted Christ, his wife trusted Christ and his kids trusted Christ. Guess what? He and his family ended up being missionaries, teaching at a school for missionary kids in another country. (The school taught the children while the parents did their missionary work.)

The high school kids were "missionaries" in their classroom and because of that, their teacher became a missionary in another country. What is a way kids your age can be examples to others of how to follow Jesus?

6. Prepare for the Future

Mark 16:15—"He said to them, 'Go into all the world and preach the good news to all creation.'"

We don't know the plans God has for us in the future. But whether you go to another country, or work in your hometown, you can still be a spreader of the good news. What is one way this week you might be able to help someone learn about Jesus? (Pray for the person. Be friendly to someone who needs friends or be fair in the way you treat someone to show Jesus' love.)

Take It Another Step

Allow children to make decorative posters of one or two of the verses. Display them in your classroom.

Building a Church

Goal: To review what's been learned about missions—and have some more fun.

What Do I Need?

- 2 sets of at least 10 wooden blocks
- List of questions (see p. 100)

How Do I Do It?

- Explain that the object of the game is to build a church with blocks. First team to use all its blocks is the winning team.
- Divide your group into two teams. Teams line up on one side of the room for a relay with an adult standing at the head of each line.
- Place the blocks at the other end of the room, directly across from the teams.

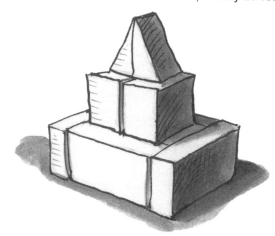

- Ask a question about missions. (As moderator, notice which children are first in line and ask questions accordingly, giving less knowledgeable children the easier questions, etc.) The child must then tell the adult the answer or asks other children to help give the answer. When the adult agrees that the correct answer has been given, the adult signals "Go." The child runs to the pile of blocks and moves one block to start the building.
- Continue playing until all blocks have been used. Repeat as time permits.

Take It Another Step

Provide children with missionary information and let them write the questions.

Learning About Missions
Building a Church Questions

1. Name a country where someone could go as a missionary.
   (Any country is correct.)

2. Name a job a missionary might have.
   (Most jobs would be correct.)

3. Name something a missionary would have to do when moving to another country.
   (Anything that makes sense such as: learn the language, get to know the people, get used to the climate, find a place to live, etc.)

4. Quote a verse about missions.
   (Any verse about telling others about Christ, working together or being kind to others.)

5. Name a missionary our church or denomination supports.

6. Name something a missionary might have to get used to when going to another country.
   (Language, culture, climate, etc.)

7. Many missionaries meet people who worship idols. Why is that a problem?
   (There is only one true God.)

8. Name a missionary in the Bible.
   (Paul, Jonah, Silas, Barnabas—others such as the disciples could also be named.)

9. Name a country where a missionary supported by our church or denomination serves.

10. Name a missionary our church or denomination supports that works right here in our country.

11. What is the most important thing a missionary does?
    (Telling others about the Lord Jesus Christ.)

12. Name a danger of being a missionary.
    (Dislike by people in the country, serving in a place where there is poor medical care, being in a country that is at war, etc.)

13. Say a word in another language.
    (Lots of children know words from television or school.)

14. What is one way a kid your age can be a missionary?
    (By telling others about the Bible, by being kind, by helping people who are in need.)

15. Why do people become missionaries?
    (Because they want to tell others about Christ.)

16. Name a missionary who has visited our church recently.

17. Name an animal a missionary might meet in another country.
    (This could be any animal.)

18. Name a food a missionary might eat in another country.
    (Any food.)

19. What can you do now to prepare to be a missionary?
    (Pray, learn about the Bible, learn to get along with other people.)

20. What does it mean to plant a church?
    (Start a church.)

Down, Down, Down (Australia)

Goal: To learn about games played by children in other countries.

What Do I Need?

- A tennis ball (or more for several groups of children to play at one time)

How Do I Do It?

- Players stand in a circle and throw a tennis ball back and forth. When a player misses the ball, all players must put one knee "down" on the ground and continue to play in that position. As the game continues, additional misses result in other body parts being placed on the ground.

> First miss—one knee
> Second miss—the other knee
> Third miss—an elbow
> Fourth miss—the other elbow
> Fifth miss—the chin

Take It Another Step

Collect information about Australia. Talk with children about the country. Ask questions ("Where is it? What is life like there? What cities are in Australia?") to see how much information children know. Give additional information as needed.

Learning About Missions
Caught You! (China)

Goal: To learn about games played by children in other countries. (This game is good for a large group.)

What Do I Need?

- A tennis ball

How Do I Do It?

- Children sit in a circle. One child is chosen to be "It" and sits outside the circle with his or her back to the group. (Make sure child can't see what is happening in the group.)
- Give the ball to any child. When the teacher says "Go," children quickly pass the ball around the circle.
- After 10 to 15 seconds, the child who is "It" says "Stop!" Whoever has the ball has to stand up and then complete an action (do five jumping jacks, sing a song, whistle, say a Bible verse, etc.).
- The child who "performs" is the next "It".

Take It Another step

Collect information about China. Talk with children about the country. Ask questions ("Where is it? What is life like there? What cities are in China?") to see how much information children know. Give additional information as needed.

Learning About Missions

Chained Words (Romania)

Goal: To learn about games played by children in other countries. (This game is good for a large group.)

What Do I Need?

- Paper and marker

How Do I Do It?

- Children sit in a circle. The first child says any word. Print the word on paper. The next child must say the first word and then a second word starting with the last two letters of the first word. (Note: For younger children, simplify the game by using only the last letter of the first word.)

> ### For instance:
> First child: Church
> Second child: Cheese
> Third child: Sentence
> Fourth child: Ceiling

- Print words on paper to help children correctly identify the last two letters of each word. The game stops when a child gets stuck.
- The next child begins a new word.

Take It Another Step

Collect information about Romania. Talk with children about the country. Ask questions ("Where is it? What is life like there? What cities are in Romania?") to see how much information children know. Give additional information as needed.

103

Big Snake (Ghana)

Goal: To learn about games played by children in other countries. (You'll need to play this game in a fairly large room.)

What Do I Need?

- No supplies needed for this activity

How Do I Do It?

- One person is "It" and chases the others. Once "It" tags someone, they hold hands to form the Big Snake, and chase someone else. When the next person is tagged, all three players grab hands and continue chasing other players. Only the first person and last person in the Big Snake can tag players.

Take It Another Step

Collect information about Ghana. Talk with children about the country. Ask questions ("Where is it? What is life like there? What cities are in Ghana?") to see how much information children know. Give additional information as needed.

Learning the Books

Goal: To learn more about the books of the Bible so children can:

1. Find a specific verse.
2. Become more knowledgeable about the Bible in general.
3. Understand a little of the chronology of the Bible (although not all books are in chronological order).

What Do I Need?

- Bibles
- A set of the Bible Book Cards (see pp. 106-114)
- Card stock
- Clear Con-Tact paper or access to a laminator

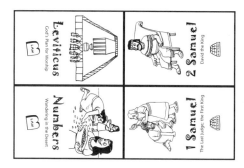

How Do I Do It?

- Copy Bible Book Cards onto card stock.
- Cover with the Con-Tact paper or laminate.
- Keep the cards in your classroom so they're handy when you have extra time.
- Choose one of the games on pages 115-119 to familiarize the kids with the books.

Take It Another Step

Give the children the opportunity to make their own sets of cards. Provide small index cards, markers and pens. Bring large envelopes for each of the children so they can work on this project over several weeks.

Bible Book Cards

How to Prepare Bible Book Cards

1. Photocopy pages 106-114 onto card stock or construction paper.

2. Laminate or cover pages with clear Con-Tact paper.

3. Cut cards apart using paper cutter or scissors.

4. Store cards in large manila envelope or resealable plastic bag.

Tips

1. Prepare several sets of cards for use in your classroom.

2. You may want to prepare a set of cards for each student to take home and use in reviewing Bible books.

3. Photocopy game directions and store them along with the appropriate Bible Book Card sets in envelopes or bags.

4. Invite volunteers to color cards with fine-tip markers before covering with Con-Tact paper.

Leviticus
God's Plan for Worship
 LAW

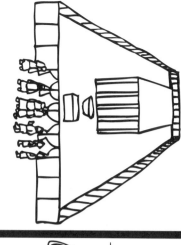

2 Samuel
David the King
HISTORY

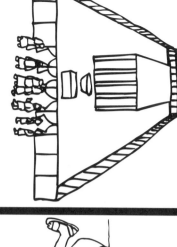

Numbers
Wandering in the Desert
LAW

1 Samuel
The Last Judge; the First King
 HISTORY

Deuteronomy
Reminders of the Law
LAW

Ruth
True Loyalty
 HISTORY

Joshua
Into the Promised Land
 HISTORY

Judges
Leaders of God's People
 HISTORY

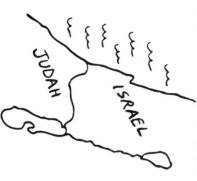

1 Kings
The Kingdom Divides

HISTORY

JUDAH
ISRAEL

Job
When Trouble Comes

POETRY

2 Kings
Kings and Prophets

HISTORY

Esther
A Queen's Bravery

HISTORY

1 Chronicles
David's Kingdom

HISTORY

Nehemiah
Rebuilding the Walls

HISTORY

2 Chronicles
Solomon and the Kings of Judah

HISTORY

Ezra
Return to Jerusalem

HISTORY

Psalms
Poems, Prayers and Songs
POETRY

Ezekiel
Strengthened by God

MAJOR PROPHETS

Proverbs
A Word to the Wise
POETRY

Lamentations
Prayers of Sadness
MAJOR PROPHETS

Ecclesiastes
The True Source of Wisdom
POETRY

Jeremiah
God's Future for Israel

MAJOR PROPHETS

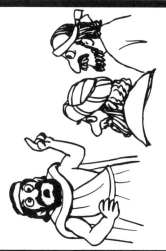

Song of Songs
Royal Love Songs

POETRY

Isaiah
God's Plan for Salvation
MAJOR PROPHETS

To us a child is born.

Daniel — Courage to Obey (MAJOR PROPHETS)

Nahum — God's Justice and Love (MINOR PROPHETS)

Hosea — A Picture of God's Love (MINOR PROPHETS)

Micah — Judgment and Hope (MINOR PROPHETS)

The Lord has a case against His people.

Joel — Past Failures and Future Promises (MINOR PROPHETS)

Jonah — God's Mercy to All People (MINOR PROPHETS)

Amos — Warnings Against Sin (MINOR PROPHETS)

Hear this word…

Obadiah — Israel Will Triumph (MINOR PROPHETS)

Habakkuk
A Conversation with God
MINOR PROPHETS

Luke
Jesus the Son of Man
GOSPELS

Zephaniah
Sorrow and Singing
MINOR PROPHETS

Mark
Jesus the Servant
GOSPELS

Haggai
Return and Rebuild
MINOR PROPHETS

Matthew
Jesus the King
GOSPELS

Zechariah
Prepare for the King
MINOR PROPHETS
Your king is coming to you.

Malachi
Trust God for the Coming Savior
MINOR PROPHETS
The Lord you are seeking will come.

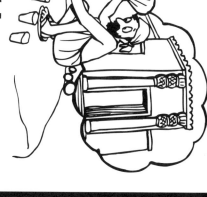

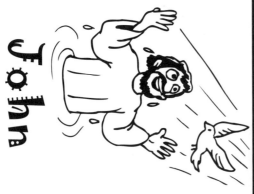

John

Jesus the Son of God

GOSPELS

Philippians

Follow Jesus in Everything

LETTERS

HISTORY

Acts

God's Family Grows

Ephesians

New Life in Christ

LETTERS

Romans

God's Amazing Grace

LETTERS

Galatians

Trust Only in Jesus

LETTERS

1 Corinthians

Living as Christians

LETTERS

2 Corinthians

Stay Away from False Teachers

LETTERS

Colossians

Christ in Charge

Hebrews

Jesus the Greatest Priest

1 Thessalonians

Jesus Our Hope

Jesus is our hope.

Philemon

A Servant Forgiven

2 Thessalonians

Jesus Will Return

Titus

Encouragement for God's Leaders

1 Timothy

Advice for Young Leaders

2 Timothy

Stand Against Persecution

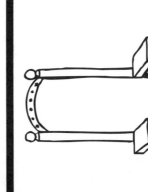

Revelation

The Return of the King

PROPHECY

James

Live Your Faith

Jude

Teach the Truth

1 Peter

Look to Jesus for Help

3 John

Be Faithful

2 Peter

All We Need in Jesus

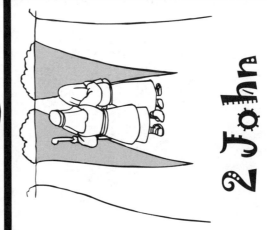

2 John

Follow Only God

1 John

Loved by God

Learning the Books
Ordering the Books

Goal: To help children learn the order of the books of the Bible

What Do I Need?

- Bibles
- A set of the Bible Book Cards (see pp. 106-114) prepared as instructed on page 106

How Do I Do It?

- Pass out a Bible Book Card to each child. If you have 12 children in your class, then give out the first 12 books (or 12 books from any section of the Bible). If your children are familiar with the books of the Bible, you may choose to give each child more than one card. Time them to see how long it takes for them to get in the right order according to their book of the Bible. Children may refer to Contents page in Bibles, as needed. Do two or three rounds of this activity and challenge them to beat their time each round.
- Keep a record of their best time in a prominent or easy-to-get-to place, so that they can continue working on breaking their record at a future date. Add additional Bible Book Cards as children increase their skills.

Take It Another Step

Change the challenge—just for fun! See how quickly the children can put themselves in alphabetical order by first or last name.

Learning the Books
Guess My Book

Goal: To help children learn information about the books of the Bible

What Do I Need?

- Bibles
- A set of the Bible Book Cards (see pp. 106-114) prepared as instructed on page 106
- Masking tape

How Do I Do It?

- Attach a Bible Book Card to the back of each child with a masking tape loop. Don't allow children to see which "book" you attached to their back. Children must ask other children "yes" or "no" questions to guess who they are. They cannot ask: "What am I about?" Or, "What person or events do I talk about in my book?" (Optional: Give quick overview of Bible books before playing this game, or choose to play game with Bible books that children have recently been studying.)

Here are some questions you could suggest to help children get started.

- Am I a book with a lot of songs in it?
- Am I a book that talks about end times?
- Was I written by Moses?
- Do you read about Jesus' miracles in me?

Take It Another Step

Child chooses a Bible Book Card and gives three clues to the group to help them guess the name of the book. Additional clues may be given as necessary. Child who guesses the book name gets to choose a card and give clues.

Learning the Books

Which Book Is It?

Goal: To help children learn information about the books of the Bible

What Do I Need?

- Two sets of the Bible Book Cards (see pp. 106-114) prepared as instructed on page 106
- Container
- Paper and pencil

How Do I Do It?

- Divide your class into two teams. Give each team the same cards both in number and book names. In other words, if you have 12 children in your class, then give each team cards for the same 12 books, etc.
- Line the teams up on opposite sides of the room. Put a container in the middle of the room. Ask the questions on the following page and see which team can find the correct Bible Book Card and run to the middle of the room and put the card into the container. Keep score.

Take It Another Step

Before placing Bible Book Cards into the container, players must perform a physical task such as 10 jumping jacks, spin around 2 times, give high-fives to everyone on their team, etc.

Learning the Books
Which Book Is It? Questions and Answers

Here are some sample questions. The most common answer is in parentheses, but children may also give additional answers to some of the questions.

- A book named for a king (Solomon)
- A book named after a lady (Esther/Ruth)
- A book whose name means "song" (Psalms)
- A book about the future (Revelation)
- A book whose name means beginning (Genesis)
- A book about a man who lost almost everything (Job)
- A book about a man who had a run-in with a fish (Jonah)
- A book about a runaway slave (Philemon)
- A book which tells us about the birth of Christ (Matthew or Luke)
- A book filled with wise sayings (Proverbs)
- A book that talks about the journey of the Israelites (Exodus)
- A book whose name means crying or sadness (Lamentations)
- A book that is a letter written to the people in Ephesus (Ephesians)
- A book that is a letter written to the people in Rome (Romans)
- The last book of the Old Testament (Malachi)
- The last book of the New Testament (Revelation)
- The book that contains the 10 Commandments (Exodus)
- One of the four gospels (Matthew, Mark, Luke or John)
- A book written by a doctor (Luke or Acts)
- A book that is a letter to a young pastor (1 or 2 Timothy)
- The next to the last book of the Bible (Jude)
- The second to the last book of the Old Testament (Zechariah)
- The second to the last book of the New Testament (Jude)
- A book written by a king (Proverbs or Song of Solomon)
- A book written by John (John, 1,2, 3 John, Revelation)
- A book that is a letter to the people of Thessalonica (1 or 2 Thessalonians)
- The book that tells us about a man thrown in a lions' den (Daniel)
- The book that tells us about John the Baptist preparing the way for Christ (John)

Hints for Learning the Books

Goal: To learn more about the books of the Bible so children can:

1. Find a specific verse.
2. Become more knowledgeable about the Bible in general.
3. Understand a little of the chronology of the Bible (although not all books are in chronological order).

What Do I Need?

- Bibles or a set of Bible Book Cards prepared as instructed on page 106
- Stopwatch (or clock with second hand)

How Do I Do It?

These are hints to teach the children to help them memorize the books of the Bible.

1. Have an ongoing contest as to who can say the books the fastest. (This is a great activity if you end up with a few extra minutes each week.) Allow children to volunteer to be part of this contest, so that you aren't putting anyone on the spot.
2. Teach the children this rhyme to help them learn how to spell Habakkuk. (And because it's fun!) See how quickly they can say it.

> H and an A and a
> B and an A and a
> K and a K and a
> U and a K

3. Help children to learn the last four books of the Old Testament by saying them as a rhyme to which they create clapping patterns in pairs.

> Zephaniah, Haggai
> Zechariah, Malachi

4. To help children learn the order of five short books in the New Testament, explain to them that five "T" books are together: 1 and 2 Thessalonians: 1 and 2 Timothy, Titus.
5. Here is a great way to help children remember how many books are in the Old Testament and how many books are in the New Testament.

> **Old Testament**
> Count: O-L-D = 3 letters
> Count: T-E-S-T-A-M-E-N-T = 9 letters
> Put 3 and 9 together and you have the number of books
> in the Old Testament.

> **New Testament**
> Count: N-E-W = 3 letters
> Count: T-E-S-T-A-M-E-N-T = 9 letters
> This time multiply 3 x 9 for a total of 27 which is the
> number of books in the New Testament.

6. To review the books of the Bible, divide into two teams. Have the first team say Genesis, the second team say Exodus, the first team say Leviticus, etc. Go back and forth. See how quickly the children can do it. (Time them to see how they can improve.)

Learning the Books
Hidden Books

Goal: To help children learn to recognize and spell the names of the books of the Bible

What Do I Need?

- A copy of A Most Silly Story (p. 121) for each child
- Pencils

How Do I Do It?

- Give a pencil and a copy of A Most Silly Story to each child.
- See how quickly children can underline or circle the names of 23 books of the Bible.

Take It Another Step

After children have completed the activity, play the game in a different way. Divide group into two teams. Teams line up across the room from a wall or table. For each team, place an enlarged copy of A Most Silly Story on the wall or table. At your signal, team members take turns running to the wall or table, marking the name of a Bible book and running back to their teams. First team to find all 23 books is the winner.

A Most Silly Story

Did you know my first job was working for Johnny Smith down at Daniel's Farm Market? When Johnny heard me, he said, "He plays the banjo elegantly. Music is in his genes, I say. I tell you the truth, I think he could play and people would stop to buy my apples, soaps, almonds and other goods."

So, my exodus from the house was early the next day. (You know the proverbs about early to bed, right?)

Johnny was already marking special prices on his fruits. Lots of numbers to count; that was a revelation. He introduced me to his dog, Tez; Ramon, his pet ermine who acts crazy, and his daughter, Judee. I liked his daughter best. Her smile was beautiful.

And what a fluke! She played banjo, too. We played and her sister Anna hummed along. (I hope no one judges our music.) We played the song of Solomon Pritchard, an old western ballad.

Even the mayor came. Timothy Mica (he's known for his unusual hose, a real clown, that man.)

Johnny sold more than ever and said he would always keep chronicles of that day.

Learning the Books

Answer Guide: A Most Silly Story

Did you know my first (job) was working for (Johnny) Smith down at (Daniel)s Farm Market? When Johnny heard me, he said, "He plays the ban(jo e)legantly. Music is in his (genes, I s)ay. I tell you the (truth) I think he could play and people would stop to buy my apples, soaps, almonds and other goods."

So, my (exodus) from the house was early the next day. (You know the (proverbs) about early to bed, right?)

Johnny was already (mark)ing special prices on his fruits. Lots of (numbers) to count; that was a (revelation). He introduced me to his dog, (Te)z; Ramon, his (pet er)mine who acts crazy, and his daughter, (Jude)e. I liked his daughter b(est. Her) smile was beautiful.

And what a (luke)! She played banjo, too. We played and her sister An(na hum)med along. (I hope no one (judges) our music.) We played the (song of Solomon) Pritchard, an old western ballad.

Even the mayor came. (Timothy)(Mica (h)e's known for his unusual (hose, a) real clown, that man.)

Johnny sold more than ever and said he would always keep (chronicles) of that day.

Memorizing a Verse

Proverbs 17:17

Goal: To memorize a verse about friendship and identify the Friendship Rule: A true friend is a friend ALL the time. (Note: There are five activities in this section. Each activity will help children identify a Friendship Rule.)

> "A friend loves at all times, and a brother is born for adversity."

What Do I Need?

- Bible

How Do I Do It?

- Read Proverbs 17:17 aloud. Ask children to tell how they would say each phrase of the verse in their own words. (You should be loyal to your friends at all times, not just when you want to go to their party or when there's no one else around to hang with. Friends are good and so is family. Families should help each other in times of trouble.)
- Tell the children to stand in a circle and then turn to the person on their right and shake their hand. Lead the children in repeating the first phrase as they shake their neighbor's hand. Do the phrase over and over. Pause and have the children shake the hand of the person on their left. Repeat the phrase again. Then ask two children to pretend they are siblings and ask them to walk in front of the other children as if one is hurt and the other one has to help him walk (by holding his elbow). (Optional: Use siblings.) Ask the siblings to walk back and forth as the children repeat the second phrase of the verse several times.
- Now, have the children say the verse all together as they shake each other's hands and the "siblings" walk back and forth, with one helping the other. (Even if the children laugh a little as they're doing this, it's OK. They'll remember the words.)

Take It Another Step

Have the children make posters of the verses and then display those posters in the room. Constantly seeing the verses will help them remember the instructions.

Memorizing a Verse
Proverbs 27:9

Goal: To memorize a verse about friendship and the Friendship Rule: A true friend gives good advice.

> "Perfume and incense bring joy to the heart, and the pleasantness of one's friend springs from his earnest counsel."

What Do I Need?

- Bible

How Do I Do It?

- Read Proverbs 27:9 aloud. Explain that the first phrase of the verse is a word picture of the "sweetness" of a friend's words. (If some children are negative about the smells of perfume and incense, suggest they think about other kinds of good smells like baking cookies or pizza.) Explain that the second phrase of the verse is talking about the helpful words we receive from friends.
- Ask children to tell examples of helpful words from friends in these situations: there's a test at school tomorrow ("Let's study for the test together."); someone has lost a cell phone ("I'm sorry you lost your phone. Let's go to the school office and see if anyone turned it in."); friends are choosing a movie to watch ("I don't think we should see that movie. I've heard it's got a lot of bad words").
- Tell the children to act as if they are smelling something good and lead them in repeating the first phrase over and over. Then as the children say the second phrase, have them crouch down and then spring up to signify the pleasantness of good advice. Repeat the verse together several times.

Take It Another Step

Review Proverbs 17:17 and the first Friendship Rule.

125

Memorizing a Verse
Proverbs 16:28

Goal: To memorize a verse about friendship and the Friendship Rule: A true friend doesn't gossip.

> "A perverse man stirs up dissension, and a gossip separates close friends."

What Do I Need?

- Bible

How Do I Do It?

- Read Proverbs 16:28 aloud. Explain that "perverse" is another word for evil and "dissension" is another word for trouble. Ask children to tell what advice about friendship this verse gives.
- Ask children to look mean and make a stirring motion as you lead them in repeating the first phrase of the verse several times. Then explain that many times when we're saying something we aren't supposed to be saying, we whisper it so no one can hear. So tell the children to whisper the last phrase of the verse. Repeat entire verse several times.

Take It Another Step

Review Proverbs 17:17; Proverbs 27:9 and the first two Friendship Rules.

Memorizing a Verse
Proverbs 19:4

Goal: To memorize a verse about friendship and the Friendship Rule: A true friend doesn't like you just to get what you have.

> "Wealth brings many friends, but a poor man's friend deserts him."

What Do I Need?

- Bible
- Optional—coins

How Do I Do It?

- Read Proverbs 19:4 aloud. Discuss the first phrase of this verse with children by explaining that sometimes a person wants to be friends with someone else because he or she wants what that person has. Ask children to tell an example or two of when kids their age might act in this way. (Kids who want to be friends with someone who has a swimming pool or a cool video game. Kids who want to be friends with a sports star or other celebrity.)
- Read the second phrase of the verse aloud. Have volunteers tell examples of when kids their age might choose NOT to be a friend with someone who doesn't have much. (Kids who avoid someone whose clothes aren't very nice, or who doesn't have money to do fun things.)
- As you lead children in repeating the first phrase of the verse, have them pretend they're counting money or jingling coins in their hands. (Optional: Use real coins.) Say the phrase several times. Then, as children repeat the second phrase, have them turn around as if they're getting ready to walk away. Repeat entire verse several times.

Take It Another Step

Review Proverbs 17:17; Proverbs 27:9; Proverbs 16:28 and the first three Friendship Rules. Children may also create their own motions for the verses.

Memorizing a Verse
Proverbs 27:17

Goal: To memorize a verse about friendship and the Friendship Rule: A true friend helps you.

> "As iron sharpens iron, so one man sharpens another."

What Do I Need?

- Bible
- Knife sharpener and knife (Make sure to keep the knife out of the reach of children.)

How Do I Do It?

- Read Proverbs 27:17 aloud. Explain that the first phrase of this verse is a word picture of a knife (or other tool) being sharpened as it is rubbed against the knife sharpener. The sharper the knife becomes, the more useful it is. Demonstrate using the knife sharpener and knife.
- Read the second phrase of the verse aloud. Discuss this phrase with children by explaining that true friends can depend on each other to help them. Ask children to suggest examples of times kids their age can help each other. (Tell a friend a way to kick a soccer ball better. Help a friend with a chore like raking the yard. Do things together to show love for God and others like helping an older person, being friendly to new kids at church or school.)

- As you lead children in saying the first phrase of the verse over and over, have them pretend to be using the knife sharpener to sharpen a knife. As children say the second phrase, have them count their fingers as if counting the useful projects they can do with their friends. (Children count a finger as they say each word of the phrase.) Repeat the entire verse several times.

Take It Another Step

Review Proverbs 17:17; Proverbs 27:9; Proverbs 16:28 and Proverbs 19:4 and the first four Friendship Rules.

Playing Some Ball

Goal: To provide a game where children can move around, and learn about the Bible.

What Do I Need?

- Bible
- One of the Questions and Answers pages from pages 130-139
- Four sheets of paper or four chairs to represent home plate, first base, second base and third base
- Scoreboard (whiteboard or large sheet of paper and marker, or chalkboard and chalk)
- Small prizes

How Do I Do It?

- Divide your class into teams and give them a minute or two to come up with team names.
- Explain the rules of the game. Bible baseball is played like regular baseball. A player comes up to the plate and chooses what level of question he or she wants: a single, double, triple or home run. The question for a double is more difficult than the question for a single, etc. Pitcher (teacher) reads the question. If the player answers the question correctly, he or she runs to the appropriate base. If the question is not answered correctly, the team gets an out. When the team receives three outs, the other team comes up to bat. (Be ready to use one of the Easy Fill-in Questions for children who continually make outs.)
- Lead children to play game as time permits. Reward the winning team with a small prize.

Take It Another Step

Make up questions as needed. (Have a Bible handy!) Or have children make up questions.

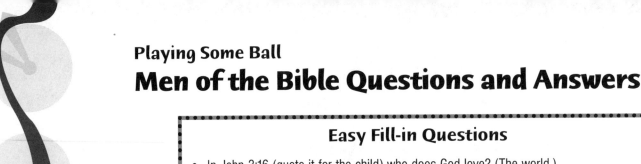

Men of the Bible Questions and Answers

Easy Fill-in Questions

- In John 3:16 (quote it for the child) who does God love? (The world.)
- In Romans 3:23 tells us (quote it for the child) how many people have sinned? (All.)
- God's Word is called what? (The Bible.)

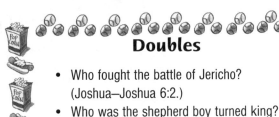

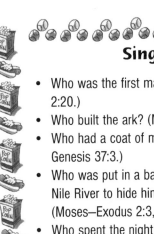

Singles

- Who was the first man? (Adam—Genesis 2:20.)
- Who built the ark? (Noah—Genesis 6:13-14.)
- Who had a coat of many colors? (Joseph—Genesis 37:3.)
- Who was put in a basket and placed in the Nile River to hide him from the Pharaoh? (Moses—Exodus 2:3,10.)
- Who spent the night with lions? (Daniel—Daniel 6:16.)

Doubles

- Who fought the battle of Jericho? (Joshua—Joshua 6:2.)
- Who was the shepherd boy turned king? (David—1 Samuel 16:13.)
- Who did David kill with a slingshot? (Goliath—1 Samuel 21:9.)
- Who was swallowed by a fish because he disobeyed God? (Jonah—Jonah 1:17.)
- Who met Jesus on the road to Damascus? (Saul [Paul]—Acts 9:3.)

Triples

- Whose wife turned into a pillar of salt? (Lot—Genesis 19:26.)
- Who was the first king of Israel? (Saul—1 Samuel 13:1.)
- Who was the wisest man in the Bible? (Solomon—1 Kings 4:30.)
- What were the names of the three men thrown into the fiery furnace? (Shadrach, Meshach and Abednego—Daniel 3:16.)
- Who denied Christ three times before the rooster crowed? (Peter—Matthew 26:75.)

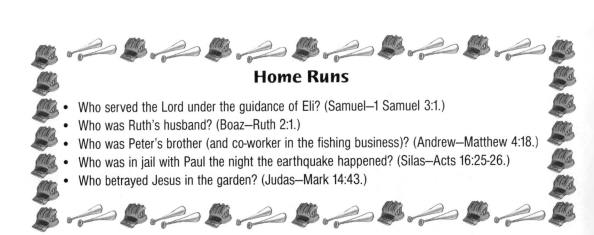

Home Runs

- Who served the Lord under the guidance of Eli? (Samuel—1 Samuel 3:1.)
- Who was Ruth's husband? (Boaz—Ruth 2:1.)
- Who was Peter's brother (and co-worker in the fishing business)? (Andrew—Matthew 4:18.)
- Who was in jail with Paul the night the earthquake happened? (Silas—Acts 16:25-26.)
- Who betrayed Jesus in the garden? (Judas—Mark 14:43.)

Playing Some Ball

Books of the Bible Questions and Answers

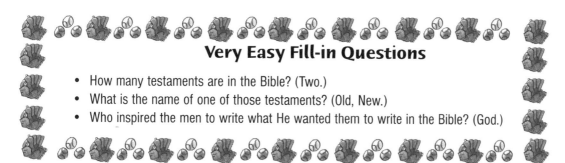

Very Easy Fill-in Questions

- How many testaments are in the Bible? (Two.)
- What is the name of one of those testaments? (Old, New.)
- Who inspired the men to write what He wanted them to write in the Bible? (God.)

Singles

- What is the first book in the Bible? (Genesis.)
- What is the last book in the Bible? (Revelation.)
- What is the first book of the New Testament? (Matthew.)
- What is the second book of the Bible? (Exodus.)
- Name one of the men whom God used to write the Bible. (Any of several answers.)

Doubles

- Name two books of the Bible that start with the letter "M." (Micah, Malachi, Matthew, Mark.)
- Name two books of the Bible that start with the letter "J." (Joshua, Judges, Job, Joel, Jonah, John, James, 1 John, 2 John, 3 John, Jude.)
- Name three books of the Old Testament. (Any three Old Testament books.)
- Name three books of the New Testament. (Any three New Testament books.)
- Who wrote the book of Revelation? (John.)

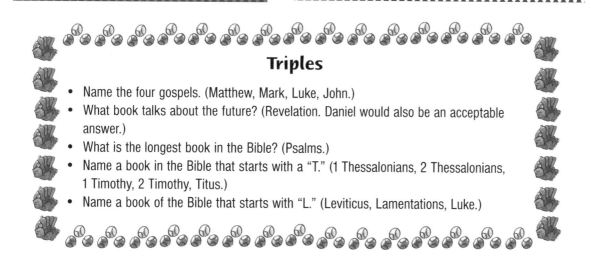

Triples

- Name the four gospels. (Matthew, Mark, Luke, John.)
- What book talks about the future? (Revelation. Daniel would also be an acceptable answer.)
- What is the longest book in the Bible? (Psalms.)
- Name a book in the Bible that starts with a "T." (1 Thessalonians, 2 Thessalonians, 1 Timothy, 2 Timothy, Titus.)
- Name a book of the Bible that starts with "L." (Leviticus, Lamentations, Luke.)

Home Runs

- How many books are in the Bible? (66.)
- How many books are in the Old Testament? (39.)
- How many books are in the New Testament? (27.)
- Name three men God used to write the Bible. (Any of several answers.)
- Name one of the two books in the Bible that are named after women. (Ruth, Esther.)

131

Women of the Bible Questions and Answers

Very Easy Fill-in Questions

- Who was the mother of Jesus? (Mary—Luke 2:5.)
- Who was the first woman? (Eve—Genesis 3:20.)

Singles

- In what town did Mary have her baby? (Bethlehem—Luke 2:4.)
- What was the name of Mary's husband? (Joseph—Luke 2:4.)
- What was the name of Abraham's wife? (Sarah—Genesis 17:15.)
- Name one of the two ladies who has a book of the Bible named after her. (Ruth or Esther.)
- Lazarus had two sisters. One was named Mary and the other was named what? (Martha—Luke 10:38.)

Doubles

- What is the name of the lady who became queen and had a Bible book written about her life? (Esther—Esther 1:7.)
- What was the name of the lady who tricked Samson? (Delilah—Judges 16:4.)
- What is the name of Naomi's daughter-in-law? (Ruth—Ruth 1:8.)
- What is the name of Isaac's wife? (Rebekah—Genesis 24:67.)
- What was the name of Rachel's sister? (Leah—Genesis 29:16.)

Triples

- What is the name of Samuel's mother? (Hannah—1 Samuel 1:20.)
- What is the name Ruth's mother-in-law? (Naomi—Ruth 1:8.)
- What is the name of John the Baptist's mother? (Elizabeth—Luke 1:5.)
- What is the name of Moses' sister? (Miriam—Exodus 15:20.)
- What is the name of lady who was David's wife and Solomon's mother? (Bathsheba—1 Kings 1:11.)

Home Runs

- What is the name of the woman who helped the spies in Jericho? (Rahab—Joshua 2:1.)
- What color cloth, fit for a king, did Lydia sell? (Purple—Acts 16:14.)
- What is the name of Aquila's wife? This couple helped Paul make tents. (Priscilla—Acts 18:2.)
- What is the name of the lady judge? (Deborah—Judges 4:4.)
- What was the name of the lady who spent her days at the Temple? She was able to hold the baby Jesus. (Anna—Luke 2:36.)

Playing Some Ball
Livin' the Life Questions and Answers

Very Easy Fill-in Questions

- Does the Bible say children should obey or disobey their parents? (Ephesians 6:1.)
- What does it mean to honor your parents? (Ephesians 6:2—to respect, love, obey.)

Singles

- Name one of the Ten Commandments. (All listed in Exodus 20.)
- Fill in the blank: According to Ephesians 6:1, children are to obey their _____.
- Fill in the blank: According to Psalm 23 the Lord is our _____ because we are His sheep.
- Of the ten men cured of leprosy, how many came back to thank Jesus? (One—Luke 17:16.)
- Name one of the characteristics of the fruit of the Spirit. (Love, joy, peace, patience, kindness, goodness, faithfulness—Galatians 5:22-23.)

Doubles

- Fill in the blank: We are to love our neighbors as we love _____. (Luke 10:27.)
- Name two men in the Bible who disobeyed God. (Many names could be used in answer to this question: Adam, Cain, Jonah, David, etc.)
- Why were Joseph's brothers jealous of him? (His father gave him a special coat—Genesis 37:2.)
- Name two of the characteristics of the fruit of the Spirit. (Love, joy, peace, patience, kindness, goodness, faithfulness—Galatians 5:22-23.)
- What was the first sin? (Adam and Eve eating the fruit God had said not to eat—Genesis 3:6.)

Triples

- Name three of the Ten Commandments. (All listed in Exodus 20.)
- Name four parts of the fruit of the Spirit. (Love, joy, peace, patience, kindness, goodness, faithfulness—Galatians 5:22-23.)
- What are we told to do in Mark 16:15? Go into all the world and _____ __ ____ __ ___ _____ (Preach the gospel to all creation.)
- What was the first murder in the Bible? (Cain killed Abel—Genesis 4:8.)
- What does it mean to covet? (To want what someone else has, to be envious, jealous—Exodus 20:17.)

Home Runs

- Name four of the Ten Commandments. (All listed in Exodus 20.)
- Name five parts of the fruit of the Spirit. (Love, joy, peace, patience, kindness, goodness, faithfulness—Galatians 5:22-23.)
- What is the first commandment with a promise? (Honor your father and mother—Ephesians 6:2.)
- Name one of the two things Paul and Silas were doing at midnight when the earthquake hit the jail where they were prisoners? (Praying and singing—Acts 16:25.)
- In Philippians we read we aren't to be anxious for anything, but instead what ARE we supposed to do? (By prayer and petition, with thanksgiving, present your requests to God—Philippians 4:6.)

133

Kings and Queens Questions and Answers

Very Easy Fill-in Questions

- The book of Esther is named after what queen? (Esther.)
- How do you spell King David? (K-I-N-G D-A-V-I-D.)

Singles

- What is the name of the shepherd boy turned king? (David—2 Samuel 2:11.)
- What was the name of the giant that David killed with his slingshot? (Goliath— 1 Samuel 17.)
- Where in the Bible can we read many of the songs that David wrote? (Psalm.)
- Who was the king who ordered all the babies killed at the time of Jesus' birth in Bethlehem? (Herod—Matthew 2:13.)
- What did King Herod tell the magi to do when they found the baby? (To come back and tell him where the baby was, so he could also go worship Him—Matthew 2:8.)

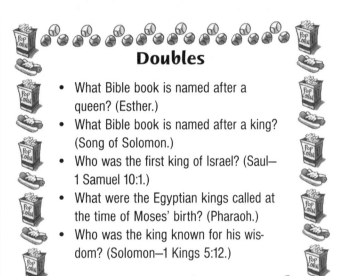

Doubles

- What Bible book is named after a queen? (Esther.)
- What Bible book is named after a king? (Song of Solomon.)
- Who was the first king of Israel? (Saul— 1 Samuel 10:1.)
- What were the Egyptian kings called at the time of Moses' birth? (Pharaoh.)
- Who was the king known for his wisdom? (Solomon—1 Kings 5:12.)

Triples

- What was the name of the Queen who visited King Solomon to see his riches? (Queen of Sheba— 1 Kings 10:1.)
- What queen scared Elijah so much that he ran away? (Jezebel—1 Kings 19:1-3.)
- What was the name of the Babylonian king who made a 90-foot high statue? (Nebuchadnezzar— Daniel 2:46.)
- Who was Absalom's father? (David—2 Samuel 3:3.)
- Who was the godly king who reigned in Judah for more than 30 years? (Josiah—2 Chronicles 34:1-3.)

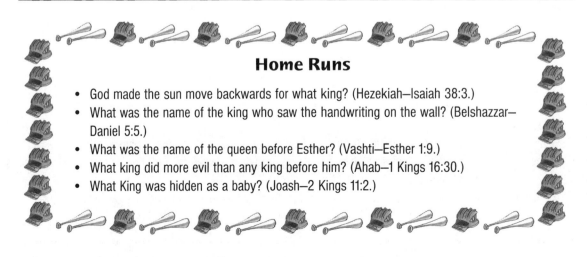

Home Runs

- God made the sun move backwards for what king? (Hezekiah—Isaiah 38:3.)
- What was the name of the king who saw the handwriting on the wall? (Belshazzar— Daniel 5:5.)
- What was the name of the queen before Esther? (Vashti—Esther 1:9.)
- What king did more evil than any king before him? (Ahab—1 Kings 16:30.)
- What King was hidden as a baby? (Joash—2 Kings 11:2.)

Playing Some Ball
Genesis Questions and Answers

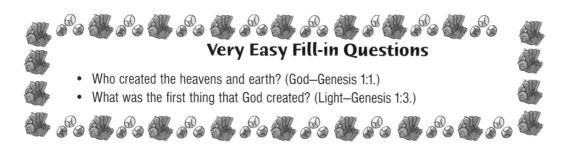

Very Easy Fill-in Questions

- Who created the heavens and earth? (God—Genesis 1:1.)
- What was the first thing that God created? (Light—Genesis 1:3.)

Singles

- What did God create on the third day of creation? (Dry land, plants and trees—Genesis 1:10-11.)
- What was the name of the first man and women? (Adam and Eve—Genesis 3:20.)
- Who built the ark? (Noah—Genesis 6:13-14.)
- What was Noah to take in the ark? (Two of every kind of animal [some children may know that he was to take seven of the clean animals]—Genesis 7:2.)
- What was the first sin? (Adam and Eve eating of the Tree of the Knowledge of Good and Evil—Genesis 2:17.)

Doubles

- After each day of creation, God "saw" what? (That it was good—Genesis 1:10.)
- How long did it rain while Noah and his family were in the ark? (Forty days and nights—Genesis 7:12.)
- What was the name of Abraham's wife? (Sarah—Genesis 17:15.)
- What did God promise Abraham and Sarah? (A baby—Genesis 17:16.)
- What was the name of Abraham and Sarah's son? (Isaac—Genesis 17:19.)

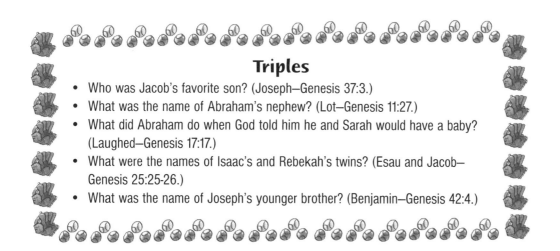

Triples

- Who was Jacob's favorite son? (Joseph—Genesis 37:3.)
- What was the name of Abraham's nephew? (Lot—Genesis 11:27.)
- What did Abraham do when God told him he and Sarah would have a baby? (Laughed—Genesis 17:17.)
- What were the names of Isaac's and Rebekah's twins? (Esau and Jacob—Genesis 25:25-26.)
- What was the name of Joseph's younger brother? (Benjamin—Genesis 42:4.)

Home Runs

- What were the names of Noah's three sons? (Shem, Ham and Japheth—Genesis 6:10.)
- What happened to Lot's wife? (She turned into a pillar of salt—Genesis 19:26.)
- What was the name of the tower the people wanted to build to the sky? (Babel—Genesis 11:9.)
- In whose house did Joseph serve? (Potiphar's—Genesis 39:1.)
- How many years of famine were there in Egypt? (Seven—Genesis 41:36.)

135

The Israelites Questions and Answers

Very Easy Fill-in Questions

- What Testament has more books, the Old or the New? (Old.)
- What is the first event talked about in Genesis? (Creation.)

Singles

- Which baby was hidden in the Nile river? (Moses–Exodus 2:10.)
- Who found Baby Moses? (Pharaoh's daughter–Exodus 2:5.)
- What was the name of the sea that God parted for the fleeing Israelites? (Red Sea–Exodus 13:18.)
- What happened when Pharaoh's army tried to get across the Red Sea? (They drowned–Exodus 15:4.)
- What did God give Moses on Mount Sinai? (The Ten Commandments–Exodus 34:28.)

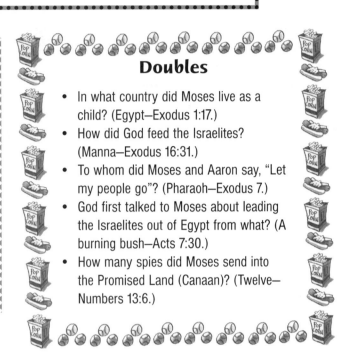

Doubles

- In what country did Moses live as a child? (Egypt–Exodus 1:17.)
- How did God feed the Israelites? (Manna–Exodus 16:31.)
- To whom did Moses and Aaron say, "Let my people go"? (Pharaoh–Exodus 7.)
- God first talked to Moses about leading the Israelites out of Egypt from what? (A burning bush–Acts 7:30.)
- How many spies did Moses send into the Promised Land (Canaan)? (Twelve–Numbers 13:6.)

Triples

- What is the name of the man who lost almost everything he had, but still remained faithful to God? (Job.)
- What was the name of Moses' brother and sister? (Aaron and Miriam–Numbers 12:4.)
- What was the first plague? (Water turned to blood–Exodus 7:20.)
- What did Aaron make for the people while Moses was on Mount Sinai? (A golden calf–Exodus 32:4.)
- What were the names of the two spies who came back with good reports? (Joshua and Caleb–Numbers 14:6-7.)

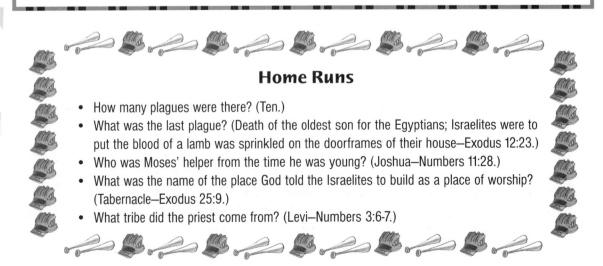

Home Runs

- How many plagues were there? (Ten.)
- What was the last plague? (Death of the oldest son for the Egyptians; Israelites were to put the blood of a lamb was sprinkled on the doorframes of their house–Exodus 12:23.)
- Who was Moses' helper from the time he was young? (Joshua–Numbers 11:28.)
- What was the name of the place God told the Israelites to build as a place of worship? (Tabernacle–Exodus 25:9.)
- What tribe did the priest come from? (Levi–Numbers 3:6-7.)

Playing Some Ball
Old Testament Questions and Answers

Very Easy Fill-in Questions

- Who was swallowed by a fish? (Jonah.)
- Who was thrown into the lion's den? (Daniel.)

Singles

- What city did God tell Joshua and his army to march around, blowing ram horns? (Jericho—Joshua 6:2.)
- Who was the little boy who helped Eli at the tabernacle? (Samuel—1 Samuel 3:1.)
- Why was Daniel thrown into the lion's den? (Because he prayed to God—Daniel 6:7.)
- What happened when Daniel was thrown into the lion's den? (God shut the lions' mouths—Daniel 6:22.)
- Who was the beautiful girl who became queen and saved the Jewish people? (Esther—Esther 2:7.)

Doubles

- Who was the strongest man in the Bible? (Samson—Judges 14:6.)
- What was the name of David's friend, Saul's son? (Jonathan—1 Samuel 13:16; 1 Samuel 18:3.)
- God talked to Balaam through what? (A donkey—Numbers 22:28.)
- What did Solomon build? (Temple—1 Kings 6:12.)
- Who was the oldest man in the Bible? (Methuselah—Genesis 5:27.)

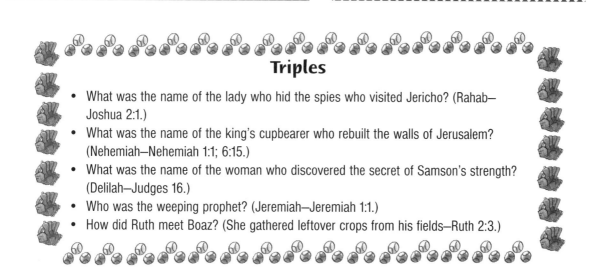

Triples

- What was the name of the lady who hid the spies who visited Jericho? (Rahab—Joshua 2:1.)
- What was the name of the king's cupbearer who rebuilt the walls of Jerusalem? (Nehemiah—Nehemiah 1:1; 6:15.)
- What was the name of the woman who discovered the secret of Samson's strength? (Delilah—Judges 16.)
- Who was the weeping prophet? (Jeremiah—Jeremiah 1:1.)
- How did Ruth meet Boaz? (She gathered leftover crops from his fields—Ruth 2:3.)

Home Runs

- What Israelite tried to "bury" his sin by hiding what he had stolen? (Achan—Joshua 7:21.)
- For whom did God allow the sun to stand still? (Joshua—Joshua 10:12.)
- What lady judge helped Barak? (Deborah—Judges 4:4-10.)
- Who was threshing wheat in a wine-press when an angel visited him? (Gideon—Judges 6:11.)
- Who went to Bethlehem to anoint the new king who was one of Jesse's sons? (Samuel—1 Samuel 16:13.)

Christmas Questions and Answers

Very Easy Fill-in Questions

- What was the name of Jesus' mother? (Mary.)
- What was the name of Jesus' earthly father? (Joseph.)

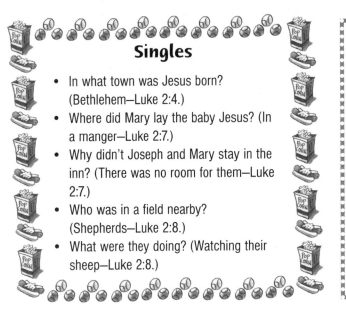

Singles

- In what town was Jesus born? (Bethlehem—Luke 2:4.)
- Where did Mary lay the baby Jesus? (In a manger—Luke 2:7.)
- Why didn't Joseph and Mary stay in the inn? (There was no room for them—Luke 2:7.)
- Who was in a field nearby? (Shepherds—Luke 2:8.)
- What were they doing? (Watching their sheep—Luke 2:8.)

Doubles

- What was the name of the angel who spoke to Mary? (Gabriel—Luke 1:26.)
- True or false: The wisemen came to the manger? (False. They came their house—Matthew 2:11.)
- What did the magi see that showed them that the "King of the Jews" had been born? (A star—Matthew 2:2.)
- Who appeared to the shepherds? (Angels—Luke 2:9.)
- Where did Mary and Joseph live? (Nazareth—Luke 1:26.)

Triples

- Who were John the Baptist's parents? (Zechariah and Elizabeth—Luke 1:5,60.)
- What gifts did the wise men bring? (Gold, incense, myrrh—Matthew 2:11.)
- What did the angels say to the shepherds? ("Glory to God in the highest, and on earth peace to men on whom his favor rests" Luke 2:14.)
- What did the shepherds do after the angels spoke to them? (They went to Bethlehem to find Joseph and Mary—Luke 2:15.)
- What were Herod's plans IF he had found the child Jesus? (He would've killed Him—Matthew 2:13.)

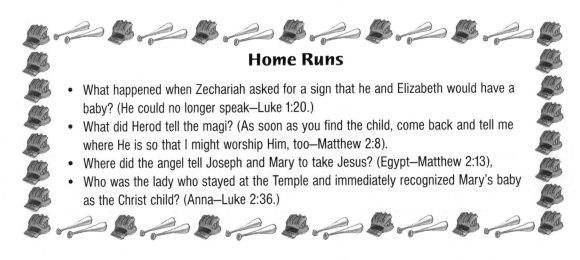

Home Runs

- What happened when Zechariah asked for a sign that he and Elizabeth would have a baby? (He could no longer speak—Luke 1:20.)
- What did Herod tell the magi? (As soon as you find the child, come back and tell me where He is so that I might worship Him, too—Matthew 2:8).
- Where did the angel tell Joseph and Mary to take Jesus? (Egypt—Matthew 2:13),
- Who was the lady who stayed at the Temple and immediately recognized Mary's baby as the Christ child? (Anna—Luke 2:36.)

Playing Some Ball
New Testament Questions and Answers

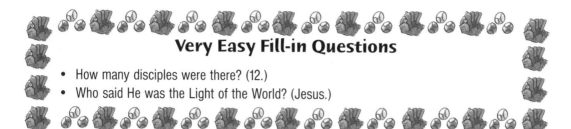

Very Easy Fill-in Questions

- How many disciples were there? (12.)
- Who said He was the Light of the World? (Jesus.)

Singles

- According to John 3:16, who does God love? (The world—John 3:16.)
- Name two of the of the four fishermen who became disciples of Jesus (Simon Peter, Andrew, James, John—Matthew 4:18-22; Mark 1:16- 34; Luke 4:33-5:11.)
- What was in the boy's lunch that Jesus used to feed the crowd of people? (Five loaves, two fish—Matthew 14:14-23.)
- What do we call a story that Jesus told? (Parable.)
- Who climbed a tree to see Jesus? (Zacchaeus—Luke 19:4.)

Doubles

- How much food was left over after Jesus fed the 5,000 men and their families? (Twelve baskets—Matthew 14:13-23.)
- Who tempted Jesus in the wilderness? (Satan—Matthew 4:1-11.)
- What disciple tried to walk on the water? (Peter—Matthew 14:23-36.)
- What kind of tree did Zacchaeus climb? (Sycamore—Luke 19:4.)
- What did Jesus say to the disciples when they tried to keep the children away from Him? (Let the little children come to me—Mark 10:14.)

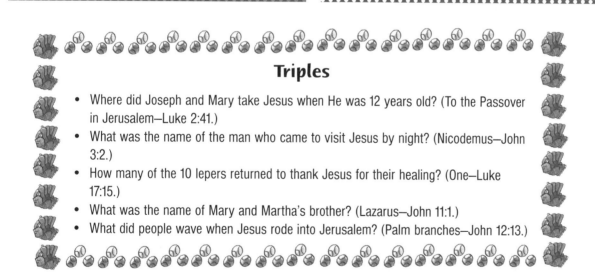

Triples

- Where did Joseph and Mary take Jesus when He was 12 years old? (To the Passover in Jerusalem—Luke 2:41.)
- What was the name of the man who came to visit Jesus by night? (Nicodemus—John 3:2.)
- How many of the 10 lepers returned to thank Jesus for their healing? (One—Luke 17:15.)
- What was the name of Mary and Martha's brother? (Lazarus—John 11:1.)
- What did people wave when Jesus rode into Jerusalem? (Palm branches—John 12:13.)

Home Runs

- What did John the Baptist eat while he was in the wilderness? (Locusts and honey—Mark 1:6.)
- In what town did Jesus' first recorded miracle take place? (Cana—John 2:1.)
- What disciples were called the Sons of Thunder? (James and John—Mark 3:17.)
- Who was the doubting disciple? (Thomas—John 20:27.)
- Who cut off a soldier's ear? (Peter—John 18:26.)

139

Letters in the Lines

Playing the Games

Goal: To provide a game where children can have fun, and learn about the Bible.

What Do I Need?

- Words or phrases cut out from page 141 and placed in a small plastic container or resealable bag. (Note: Label container with lid, or bag with the name of the game and use for storage.)
- Whiteboard and markers

How Do I Do It?

- Start the game by choosing a word and drawing a line on the board to represent each letter. If the answer includes more than one word, leave an extra space between the words.
- Children take turns guessing letters. If the letter is in the word, write it in the correct space. If it isn't in the word, draw the first line of the Bible graphic (see sketch) and the incorrect letter off to the side. The goal is for the children to guess the word before the Bible is completely drawn.
- The child who gives the correct answer is the next challenger. Child can think of his or her own Bible word, or select a word from the container or bag you prepared.

Tips for Playing

- Here's a suggestion if YOU start the game. Use the word "church." It's simple, but often difficult for children to get because they guess every other vowel before "u." And, though it is a six-letter word, two letters are repeated.
- This game often stalls because children can't think of words or when they do think of words, they don't know how to spell them. Providing the words can keep the game moving and gives the child the correct spelling. If some of the words provided in the list on page 141 are too difficult for the children in your group, omit them.
- This is a game you can continue playing as parents come to pick up their children, helping to eliminate the chaos that sometimes happens at the end of class.

Take It Another Step

You may also play this game by dividing the group into teams, with teams earning points for each word guessed. Or, you may use words from Bible stories or verses children have been studying.

Game Words for Letters in the Lines

Disciple	Gethsemane	Hallelujah
Habakkuk	Aaron	Nile River
Chariot	Dove	Revelation
Silas	Serpent	Isaac
Joy	Resurrection	Tabernacle
Peace	Gospel	Joel
Timothy	Temple	Galilee
Isaiah	Grace	Amen
Jerusalem	Beatitudes	Whirlwind
Bible	Elisha	Gentleness
Boaz	Israelites	Gideon
Kingdom	Nineveh	New Testament
Nebuchadnezzar	Balaam	King Saul
Dead Sea	Mount of Olives	Leprosy
Old Testament	Altar	Nazareth
Garden of Eden	Angels	Samuel

Sketching a Scene

Goal: To provide a game where children can have fun, and learn about the Bible.

What Do I Need?

- Words or phrases cut out from page 143 and placed in a small plastic container or resealable bag. (Note: Label container with lid, or bag with the name of the game and use for storage.)
- Whiteboard and markers
- An additional whiteboard or sheet of poster board to use for scorekeeping

How Do I Do It?

- Divide group into two teams.
- A player from the first team selects a phrase from the container. The player then has one minute to draw on the whiteboard clues for his or her team to guess the phrase. When the phrase is guessed, the team is awarded 100 points. If the team doesn't guess the phrase, then the other team has 30 seconds to answer. If no one guesses the answer within that amount of time, no points are awarded.
- For the next round, the other team sends a player to draw on the board.

Take It Another Step

Use words or scenes from Bible stories children have recently studied.

Game Words for Sketching a Scene

Red Sea	Manger	Heaven
Queen Esther	Bethlehem	Noah's flood
Mount Sinai	Shepherds	King Solomon
Ten Commandments	Tree of the Knowledge of Good and Evil	Coat of many colors
Streets of gold	Daniel	New Testament
Paul and Silas	Golden calf	Ten Commandments
David and Goliath	Jonah	Lost sheep
Temple	Tower of Babel	Pillar of fire
Plague of frogs	Samson	Ark of the Covenant
Prayer	Shipwreck	Mary and Joseph
Burning bush	Five loaves and two fish	Pillar of salt
The cross	Light of the world	Missionary
Sermon on the Mount	Old Testament	Creation
Angels	Jordan River	Praising God
Harp	Jesus loves me	Manna
Blind man healed	Shadrach, Meshach and Abednego	Baby Moses

143

Playing the Game

Name the Noun

Goal: To provide a game where children can have fun, and learn about the Bible.

What Do I Need?

- Phrases and Answers for Name the Noun (p. 145)
- Small prizes

How Do I Do It?

- Divide group into two teams.
- Call out a word or first part of a phrase from page 145 and see who can come up with the word that completes the thought. For instance, if you call out "New," a child would answer "Testament." Give 10 points to the child's team.
- Continue as time permits. If one or two children are monopolizing the answers, make a rule that once you've answered a question, you need to "sit out" for the next two questions.
- Some of the adjectives will have more than one answer. Use your judgment as to whether or not to accept the answer.
- Give a small prize to each member of the winning team.

Take It Another Step

Challenge the children to come up with phrases of their own. Or, use this game to review a Bible story children have recently studied.

Phrases and Answers for Name the Noun

The answers are in parentheses.

Holy (Bible)

The patience of (Job)

Doubting (Thomas)

Last (Supper)

Sermon on the (Mount)

Ten (Commandments)

Daniel and the (lions' den)

Noah's (ark)

Garden of (Eden)

For God so loved (the world)

The Good (Samaritan)

For all have (sinned)

Mary and (Joseph)

The Fruit of (the Spirit)

Red (Sea)

God saw that (it was good)

The Lord is (my shepherd)

Queen of (Sheba)

David and (Goliath)

Matthew, Mark, Luke and (John)

Children, obey (your parents)

Glory to God in the highest (and on earth peace to men)

The Last (Supper)

Honor your (father and your mother)

John the (Baptist)

Love (your neighbor)

Alpha (and Omega)

Jacob (and Esau)

Song of (Solomon)

I am the Bread of (life)

Love the Lord your God with (all your heart)

Abraham and (Sarah)

Sodom and (Gomorrah)

Sea of (Galilee)

Let my people (go)

Adam and (Eve)

Street of (gold)

Ark of the (Covenant)

Give us today (our daily bread)

Aquila and (Priscilla)

Walls of (Jericho)

The gift of God is (eternal life)

Playing the Games

Role Plays with Real Props

Goal: To provide a game where children can have fun, and learn about the Bible.

What Do I Need?

- Enough props so you have one for each team (classroom objects, preschool toys, etc.)

How Do I Do It?

- Divide group into teams (along with an adult for each team to provide direction).
- Give each team a prop.
- Give the teams 10 minutes to plan and practice a role play using the prop that either dramatizes a Bible event or a contemporary situation that shows someone obeying a Bible verse. (Note: Depending on the age of the children in your group, and their familiarity with Bible stories, you may need to bring props for specific stories or verses [see suggestions below].)

For instance:

- Object is a basket. Children role play Jesus' miraculous feeding of the 5,000 (see Mark 6), or Moses being hidden in the basket on the river (see Exodus 2).
- Object is a purple scarf. Children role play Paul meeting Lydia and other people by the river (see Acts 16).
- Object is an MP3 player. Children role play a boy who chooses to let his sister use the MP3 player.
- Object is a dollar bill. Children role play a girl who finds the dollar bill on the school playground and turns it in to the office.
- After preparing, allow the children to do their role-plays for the other children. Have fun with this by giving teams of older children unusual objects and enjoying the resulting role plays.

Take It Another Step

Take digital photos or video the role plays.

146

Playing the Games
Living Letters

Goal: To provide a game where children can have fun, and learn about the Bible.

What Do I Need?

- Small prizes

How Do I Do It?

- Divide group into two teams.
- Have the teams stand on opposite sides of the room.
- Call out a word from a Bible verse that children have recently studied. Children spell out the letters with their bodies. For instance, if you call out the word "Joy," one child stands straight and curves one leg back to form a "J." Another child makes large circle with arms to be the "O." A third child extends arms in "V" shape to form "Y."

- Depending on word length, not every team member will be used in forming each word.
- The team who first spells the word gets a point.
- Award a small prize to each member of the winning team.
- Be prepared for a lot of laughter.

Take It Another Step

Look the words up in the Bible.

Playing the Games
Bible Story Charades

Goal: To provide a game where children can have fun, and learn about the Bible.

What Do I Need?

- Words or phrases cut out from page 149 and placed in a small plastic container or resealable bag. (Note: Label container with lid, or bag with the name of the game and use for storage.)
- Whiteboard or sheet of poster board to use for scorekeeping

How Do I Do It?

- Divide group into two teams.
- Two players from the first team select a phrase from the container (or have players select a scene from recently studied Bible stories). The players have 1 minute to act out a scene from the Bible story for their own team while the other team watches. If the team guesses the story, they are awarded 100 points. If the team doesn't guess the Bible story, then the other team has 30 seconds to guess the Bible story. If no one gets it within that amount of time, neither team receives any points.
- For the next round, the second team sends two players to select a phrase and act out a scene from the Bible story. Continue rounds as time permits.

Take It Another Step

Are some of the teams good at acting out scenes? Maybe your class could repeat their charades for another class. See how many situations the other class can identify. Or, you may videotape the charades and lay video for parents to guess the Bible stories.

Phrases for Bible Story Charades

Noah builds the ark	Caleb and Joshua return with glowing reports of the Promised Land
David defeats Goliath	Zaachaeus climbs tree to see Jesus
People build the Tower of Babel	Jesus feeds the 5,000
Israelites cross the Red Sea	Jesus calms waves in a storm
The prodigal son returns home	Rahab protects the spies
Joseph's brothers sell him to traders	Jonah is swallowed by a fish
Princess discovers baby Moses	Daniel prays
Paul and Silas sing in prison	Samuel hears God's call at night
Angels tell good news to shepherds	Saul blinded on the way to Damascus
The shepherd rescues the lost sheep	Ten lepers healed by Jesus, only one returns to say "thanks"

Playing the Games
People Tic-Tac-Toe

Goal: To provide a game where children can have fun, and learn about the Bible.

What Do I Need?

- Nine chairs
- A list of verses recently memorized in your class
- Construction paper in two colors.

How Do I Do It?

- Set the chairs in the middle of the room in three rows of three chairs each to represent a Tic-Tac-Toe board.
- Divide group into two teams. Have the teams line up facing each other an equal distance away from the Tic-Tac-Toe board. Each team needs a teacher to stand near the team.
- Assign each team a color and give each team member a sheet of paper of the appropriate color.
- Lead teams to play a game like Tic-Tac-Toe. The goal is for a team to have three of their players sit in a row either vertically, horizontally or diagonally.

- Call out the reference from a familiar Bible verse or a verse you've recently learned in class. First child on each team tries to be the first player to say the verse correctly to the teacher standing by the team, run to the Tic-Tac-Toe board and sit down on any open chair. For each reference, only the first child to reach the board is allowed to remain on the board. Continue until one team scores Tic-Tac-Toe, or until the Tic-Tac-Toe board is full. Repeat game with a different reference.

Take It Another Step

Play the game by asking questions about Bible stories children have recently studied.

Four Square Just for Fun

Goal: To have fun and use up some energy.

What Do I Need?

- A large square marked with masking tape on the floor and divided into four squares. The squares need to be marked one, two, three and four. (Or children need to know the numbers of the squares.)
- A ball

How Do I Do It?

- The first four players each stand in a separate square. The other players stand in a line waiting to get into the game.
- The player in square one drops the ball and hits it underhanded into any other square. Player in that square hits the ball underhanded into any other square.
- Play continues until someone hits the ball out of bounds or a player cannot hit the ball from his or her square into someone else's square.
- When a player misses the ball, player goes to the end of the line and everyone else moves up. The first person in line now steps into square one. Continue play as time and interest permit.

Take It Another Step

Players say words of a Bible verse in order, one word for each hit of the ball.

Animals of the Bible

Saying
the Alphabet

Goal: To name Bible animals for letters of the alphabet.
(Note: The animals listed below are based on the
New International Version of the Bible.)

What Do I Need?

- Bibles (*NIV*)
- A large sheet of paper, whiteboard or chalkboard for each team
- Markers or chalk

How Do I Do It?

- Divide your group into teams or work together as one team.
- Write the letters of the alphabet on a sheet of poster board, whiteboard or chalkboard. Assign someone (or one "writer" for each team) to write names of Bible animals as children call them out. Set a time limit. Some of the letters will be easy, others will be difficult. (Optional: Print Scripture references [see below] on slips of paper. Give an equal number of papers to each team for teams to find and read.)

Sample List:

A Ant (a wise worker) Proverbs 6:6

B Bat (example of unclean animal) Leviticus 11:19

C Camels (Queen of Sheba took camels when she visited Solomon) 1 Kings 10:2

D Donkey (one of Abraham's animals) Genesis 12:16

E Eagle (a picture of how strong we are in the Lord) Isaiah 40:31

F Falcon (bird that preys) Deuteronomy 14:13

G Goat (a picture of people who don't obey God) Matthew 25:32

H Hawk (Job describes the hawk to his friends) Job 39:26

I Ibex (a clean animal) Deuteronomy 14:5

J Jackal (Job talks about jackals to his friends) Job 30:29

K Kite (a type of bird that preys, similar to a falcon) Deuteronomy 14:13

L Leopard (word picture trying to be something you really aren't) Jeremiah 13:23

M Mule (mules were used for transportation) 2 Samuel 18:9

N No "n" animals in *NIV*

O Owl (hides in lonely places) Psalm 102:6

P Partridge (picture of a man who unfairly gets his riches) Jeremiah 17:11

Q Quail (God's meal for the Israelites) Exodus 16:13

R Rooster (Peter denies he knew Christ before the rooster crowed three times) Luke 22:34

S Sheep (word picture—The Lord is our Shepherd. We are his sheep) John 10:14

T No "T" animals in *NIV*.

U No "U" animals in *NIV*.

V Viper (grabs onto Paul's hand) Acts 28:3

W Worm (word picture of something low and hated) Psalms 22:6

X No Bible animals had names beginning with X.

Y No Bible animals had names beginning with Y.

Z No Bible animals had names beginning with Z.

Take It Another Step

Discuss some of the animals: "What was their purpose? If they were used as word pictures, what do they represent? Were they key parts of Bible events? How?"

Saying the Alphabet
Women of the Bible

Goal: To name Bible women for letters of the alphabet. (Note: The women listed below are based on the *New International Version* of the Bible.)

What Do I Need?

- Bibles (*NIV*)
- A large sheet of paper, whiteboard or chalkboard for each team
- Markers or chalk

How Do I Do It?

- Divide your group into teams or work together as one team.
- Write the letters of the alphabet on a sheet of poster board, whiteboard or chalkboard. Assign someone (or one "writer" for each team) to write names of Bible women as children call them out. Set a time limit. Some of the letters will be easy, others will be difficult. (Optional: Print Scripture references [see below] on slips of paper. Give an equal number of papers to each team for teams to find and read.)

Sample List:

A Abigail (David's wife) 2 Samuel 2:2	N Naomi (mother-in-law of Ruth) Ruth 1:8
B Bathsheba (David's wife) 2 Samuel 11:3	O Orpah (daughter-in-law of Naomi) Ruth 1:4
C Claudia (friend of Paul and Timothy) 2 Timothy 4:21	P Priscilla (tentmaker and with her husband, a friend of Paul's) Acts 18:2
D Dorcas (a woman who did good, died and came alive again) Acts 9:36	Q Queen of Sheba (visited Solomon to see his wealth and test his wisdom) 1 Kings 10:13
E Elizabeth (mother of John the Baptist) Luke 1:13	R Rachel (Jacob's wife) Genesis 29:6
F No women had names beginning with F.	S Sarah (Abraham's wife) Genesis 17:15
G Gomer (Hosea's wife) Hosea 1:3	T Tabitha (another name for Dorcas) Acts 9:36
H Hannah (mother of Samuel) 1 Samuel 1:20	U No women had names beginning with U.
I Iscah (Lot's sister) Genesis 11:29	V Vashti (queen before Esther) Esther 1:9
J Jemima (Job's daughter) Job 42:14	W No ladies had names beginning with W.
K Keturah (woman in Abraham's household) Genesis 25:1	X No ladies had names beginning with X.
L Lydia (seller of purple) Acts 16:14	Y No ladies had names beginning with Y.
M Mary (chosen to be mother of Jesus) Luke 2:16	Z Zeresh (Haman's wife) Esther 5:10

Take It Another Step

Discuss some of the women: "How did this woman show love and obedience to God? What is this woman famous for doing or saying? Who are the relatives of this woman? What did they do?"

153

Saying the Alphabet
Bible Verses

Goal: To name Bible verses beginning with letters of the alphabet. (Note: The verses listed below are from the *New International Version* of the Bible.)

What Do I Need?

- Bibles (*NIV*)
- A large sheet of paper, whiteboard or chalkboard for each team
- Markers or chalk

How Do I Do It?

- Divide your group into teams or work together as one team.
- Write the letters of the alphabet on a sheet of poster board, whiteboard or chalkboard. Assign someone (or one "writer" for each team) to write Bible verses as children call them out. Set a time limit. Some of the letters will be easy, others will be difficult. (Optional: Print Scripture references [see below] on slips of paper. Give an equal number of papers to each team for teams to find and read.)

Sample List with the First Few Words of the Verses:

A "A friend loves at all times." Proverbs 17:17
B "Be kind." Ephesians 4:32
C "Children, obey your parents." Ephesians 6:1
D "Do not be anxious about anything." Philippians 4:6
E "Enter his gates with thanksgiving." Psalm 100:4
F "For all have sinned." Romans 3:23
G "God called the light 'day.'" Genesis 1:5
H "Honor your father and your mother." Exodus 20:12
I "In the beginning." Genesis 1:1
J "Jesus answered, 'I am the way and the truth and the life.'" John 14:6
K "Know that the Lord is God." Psalms 100:3
L "Love the Lord your God with all your heart." Deuteronomy 6:5
M "Make every effort to live in peace with all men and to be holy." Hebrews 12:14
N "Now the earth was formless and empty." Genesis 1:2

O "On hearing this." Matthew 9:12
P "Pray continually." 1 Thessalonians 5:17
Q "Queen Vashti also gave a banquet for the women." Esther 1:9
R "Rejoice in the Lord always." Philippians 4:4
S "Shout for joy to the Lord, all the earth." Psalm 100:1
T "The Lord is my shepherd." Psalm 23:1
U "Unless the Lord builds the house." Psalms 127:1
V "'Very well, then,' he said, 'let it be as you say.'" Genesis 44:10
W "We all, like sheep, have gone astray." Isaiah 53:6
X No verses that begin with X.
Y "Yet to all who received him." John 1:12
Z "Zion will be redeemed with justice." Isaiah 1:27

Take It Another Step

Discuss some of the verses: "How would you say this verse in your own words? What does this verse teach us about God? What does this verse teach us about how we should act?"

Men of the Bible

Goal: To name Bible men beginning with letters of the alphabet. (Note: The men listed below are based on the *New International Version* of the Bible.)

What Do I Need?

- Bibles (*NIV*)
- A large sheet of paper, whiteboard or chalkboard for each team
- Markers or chalk

How Do I Do It?

- Divide your group into teams or work together as one team.
- Write the letters of the alphabet on a sheet of poster board, whiteboard or chalkboard. Assign someone (or one "writer" for each team) to write names of Bible men as children call them out. Set a time limit. Some of the letters will be easy, others will be difficult. (Optional: Print Scripture references [see below] on slips of paper. Give an equal number of papers to each team for teams to find and read.)

Sample List:

A Adam (first man) Genesis 2:20	O Obadiah (a prophet) Obadiah 1:1
B Barnabas (encourager, Paul's friend) Acts 9:27	P Peter (disciple of Jesus) Matthew 4:18
C David (shepherd boy to king) 1 Samuel 16:13	Q Quartus (friend of Paul's) Romans 16:23
E Eli (priest whom Samuel served) 1 Samuel 1:9	R Reuben (Jacob's firstborn son) Genesis 29:32
F Felix (governor who heard Paul) Acts 24:2	S Saul (first king of Israel) 1 Samuel 9:2
G Goliath (giant whom David killed with a slingshot) 1 Samuel 17:4	T Timothy (a pastor, Paul's friend) 1 Corinthians 4:17
H Haggai (prophet of God) Haggai 1:1	U Uriah (commander in David's army, wife of Bathsheba) 2 Samuel 11:3
J Jonah (ran away from God and was swallowed by a fish) Jonah 1:3	V Vaizatha (one of Haman's sons) Esther 9:9
K Kolaiah (father of Ahab) Jeremiah 29:21	W No men had names beginning with W.
L Luke (doctor, writer of the third book of the New Testament) Colossians 4:14	X Xerxes (King, husband of Esther) Esther 1:1
M Matthew (disciple of Jesus) Luke 6:15	Y No men had names beginning with Y.
N Noah (built an ark) Genesis 6:8	Z Zechariah (father of John the Baptist) Luke 1:5

Take It Another Step

Discuss some of the men on your list: "How did this man show love and obedience to God? What is this man famous for doing or saying? Who are the relatives of this man? What did they do?"

Saying the Alphabet
Bible Place Names

Goal: To name Bible places beginning with letters of the alphabet. (Note: The places listed below are based on the *New International Version* of the Bible.)

What Do I Need?

- Bibles (*NIV*)
- A large sheet of paper, whiteboard or chalkboard for each team
- Markers or chalk

How Do I Do It?

- Divide your group into teams or work together as one team.
- Write the letters of the alphabet on a sheet of poster board, whiteboard or chalkboard. Assign someone (or one "writer" for each team) to write names of Bible places as children call them out. Set a time limit. Some of the letters will be easy, others will be difficult. (Optional: Print Scripture references [see below] on slips of paper. Give an equal number of papers to each team for teams to find and read.)

Sample List:

A Ararat (mountain resting place of Noah's ark) Genesis 8:4

B Bethlehem (town where Christ was born) Luke 2:4

C Capernaum (town where Jesus preached during His ministry on earth) Matthew 17:24

D Damascus (Paul was traveling to Damascus when blinded) Acts 9:3

E Egypt (country where Joseph was a slave) Genesis 37:36

F Fair Havens (a harbor Paul visited on his missionary journey) Acts 27:8

G Galilee (the name of the sea where Peter and Andrew, James and John fished) Matthew 4:18

H Horeb (mountain where Moses saw the burning bush) Exodus 3:1

I India (part of the kingdom of Xerxes—Esther's king) Esther 1:1

J Jerusalem (center of Israel, its history and its future) 2 Chronicles 3:1

K Kanah (river/ravine) Joshua 16:8

L Lake of Gennesaret (another name for the Sea of Galilee) Luke 5:1

M Mount of Olives (place where Jesus was betrayed) Matthew 26:30

N Nazareth (town where Joseph and Mary were from) Luke 2:4

O Oholibah (a symbolic name for Jerusalem) Ezekiel 23:4

P Philadelphia (one of the seven churches in Revelation) Revelation 3:7

Q Qumran is not in the Bible. If you are doing this activity as a group, however, you may explain to your class that this is the place where the shepherd found the Dead Sea Scrolls.

R Rome (Paul wrote a letter to the people in the city of Rome. We call the letter "Romans." Aquila and Priscilla were from Rome.) Acts 18:2

S Samaria (capital city of the northern kingdom of Israel) 1 Kings 16:24

T Thessalonica (Paul wrote two letters to the people in the city of Thessalonica. We call those letters 1 and 2 Thessalonians.) Philippians 4:16

U Ur (city) Genesis 11:29

V Valley of Elah (where Saul and the Israelites camped) 1 Samuel 17:2

W West Gate (gate in the city of Jerusalem) 1 Chronicles 26:16

X No Bible places that start with the letter X.

Y No Bible places that start with the letter Y.

Z Zion (an area of Jerusalem) 2 Samuel 5:7

Take It Another Step

Discuss some of the places on your list: "What happened at this place? What do you learn about God from something that happened at this place?"

Saying the Alphabet
Song Titles

Goal: To name songs whose titles begin with letters of the alphabet.

What Do I Need?

- Bibles
- A large sheet of paper, whiteboard or chalkboard for each team
- Markers or chalk

How Do I Do It?

- Divide your group into teams or work together as one team.
- Write the letters of the alphabet on a sheet of poster board, whiteboard or chalkboard. Assign someone (or one "writer" for each team) to write song titles as children call them out. Set a time limit. Some of the letters will be easy, others will be difficult.

Sample List:*

A	Amazing Grace
B	B-I-B-L-E
E	Every Move I Make
F	Father Abraham
J	Jesus Loves Me
L	Lord, I Lift Your Name on High
O	Open the Eyes of My Heart, Lord
P	Pharaoh, Pharaoh
S	Shout to the Lord
T	This Little Light of Mine

Take It Another Step

Sing the songs together. For a fun option, start with the A song and each week sing the next song in the alphabet right through to Z.

* Because children in different churches sing different songs, making a sample list is difficult.

Serving Others

Toddler Concert

Goal: To encourage children to sing praise to God.

What Do I Need?

- A fun kids' song

How Do I Do It?

- Ask children to suggest several favorite songs that they think toddlers would enjoy. Then allow children to vote for their favorite song. (For each round of voting, eliminate the song that receives the fewest votes until you come up with number one.)
- Sing the song a few times.
- Talk about the importance of serving others and explain to children that singing is a way to serve.
- Send a messenger down to the toddler nursery or any class of younger children. Ask if you can bring the older children down for an impromptu concert. (If your children are getting restless because of a prolonged service, you can imagine the restlessness in the toddler nursery.)
- If you don't have time to actually sing the song to the younger class, make arrangements to visit and sing at a later date.

Take It Another Step

Provide rhythm instruments for toddlers to use to accompany the singing.

Serving Others
Clean It Up

Goal: To encourage children to help keep their classroom clean.

What Do I Need?

- Cleaning supplies (Choose child-safe supplies. Use soap and water instead of chemical cleaners.)

How Do I Do It?

- Have a ready list of those "someday-I'll-have-to" projects you plan to get done, but never do such as:
    - Scrub the scuff marks off chairs and floor. (Some of the children may remember how they got there!)
    - Clean out all those leftover, ripped paper pieces from the crayon boxes.
    - Scrub crayon marks off the tables.
    - Neaten the supply closet.
- Assign the children to different tasks. If you have a large group and a large room, assign a team of children to each task. If teachers work with the children, you may be surprised at their willingness and excitement to help. Be sure to thank the children for jobs well done. (Optional: Let parents know the ways in which their children served others.)

Take It Another Step

Ask the kids to make a list of rules to KEEP the room clean.

Serving Others
We're Authors!

Goal: To encourage older children to help younger children.

What Do I Need?

- Whiteboard or paper and markers
- Construction paper
- Pen or pencil
- Markers or crayons
- Stapler
- Optional—three-ring binder and plastic page protectors

How Do I Do It?

- Lead children to brainstorm a favorite Bible story that they think younger children will enjoy.
- Ask children to dictate story sentences. Print the sentences on whiteboard or paper.
- Assign a sentence or two to each child or pair of children. Children write sentences on paper and draw appropriate illustrations.
- Assemble the completed pages in order and staple on left side to make a book. (Optional: Put the pages in plastic-page protectors and arrange in order in a three-ring binder.) If possible, allow children to accompany you to deliver the book to a class of younger children.

Take It Another Step

Keep the book in the church library.

Serving Others
Welcome

Goal: To give children an opportunity to be part of the church welcoming committee by creating welcome letters for children's welcome packets. (Note: If your church does not already have a welcome packet for children, discuss the possibility with your children's pastor or children's ministry team. Packets typically contain a brochure on children's activities, a pencil, notepad, gum, etc.)

What Do I Need?

- Children's welcome packet, if available
- Copies of page 162
- Markers
- Pen and pencils
- Plain paper for younger children who can't write
- Crayons for younger children

How Do I Do It?

- Show a sample of a children's welcome packet. Explain to your class that the packets are given to visiting children. Ask children to tell how they felt the first time they attended church or how they felt visiting another church. Tell them that the packets help the children feel at home.
- Give each child a copy of the letter on page 162. Provide pens and pencils for children to fill in the blank spaces of the letters. Provide markers for them to decorate their letters.
- Give younger children plain paper and crayons so they can draw a "welcome" picture.
- Make sure the letters get into the welcome packs. (Sometimes class projects sit forgotten on a shelf or in a closet.)

Take It Another Step

Offer to have your class help assemble the packets.

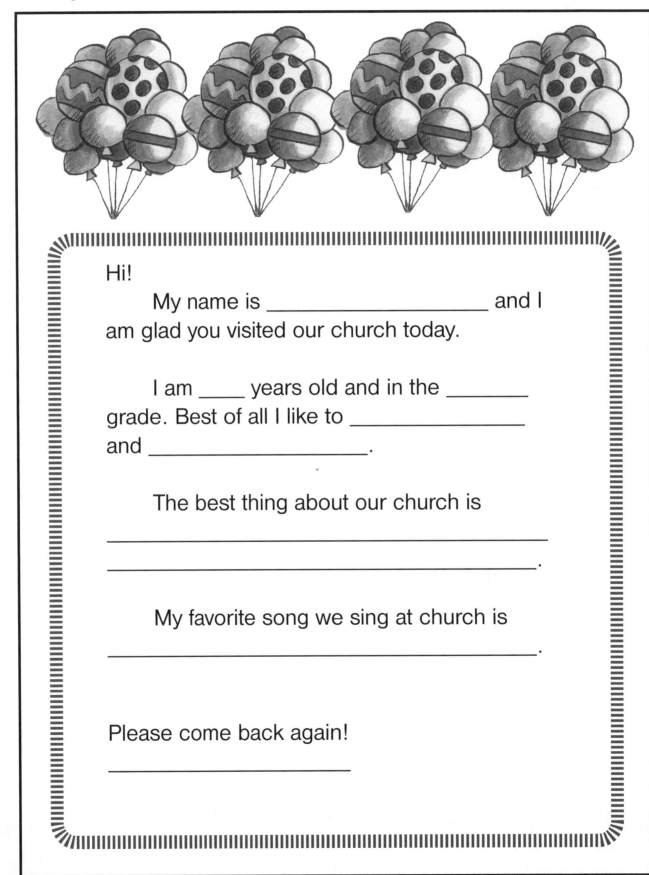

Hi!

My name is _____ and I am glad you visited our church today.

I am _____ years old and in the _____ grade. Best of all I like to _____ and _____.

The best thing about our church is

_____
_____.

My favorite song we sing at church is

_____.

Please come back again!

_____

Serving Others
Where Have You Been?

Goal: To give children an opportunity to contact absentees.

What Do I Need?

- List of absentee children
- Plain postcards (purchase at an office store or make your own from heavy paper)
- Markers
- Stamps

How Do I Do It?

- Give the children names of absentees for whom to make "We miss you" post-cards. (Hearing from another child in the class may get an absentee's attention.) More than one child may make a card for an absentee.
- Instruct the children to draw a design on the front of the card. The back of the card should be divided in half: one half for the message and one half for the address. (Children can also use the front of the card for a message.)
- Write some phrases on the board for younger children to copy.
    - We miss you.
    - Where have you been?
    - We miss your smile.
    - Come back! You're missing the fun!
- Address, stamp and mail the postcards to the absentees.

Take It Another Step

Have children design some generic postcards to be used in the future.

Serving Others
Suncatchers

Goal: To give children an opportunity to encourage the elderly or shut-ins.

What Do I Need?

- Various colors of cellophane
- Clear Con-Tact paper cut into 4-inch (10-cm) squares
- Scissors
- Hole punch
- Ribbon

How Do I Do It?

- Give the children several pieces of cellophane and have then cut or tear into pieces (approximately 1 to 2 inches [2.5 to5 cm] across). (See sketch a.)
- Give each child a piece of Con-Tact paper and instruct them to completely cover the paper with the cellophane. Pieces should overlap on the edges. (See sketch b.)
- Put a second piece of Con-Tact paper down on top of the first one. (See sketch c.) (Teachers will need to help younger children.)
- Cut a design (a heart, flower, shape, etc.) out of the finished product. (See sketch d.)
- Punch a hole in the top of the design and tie a ribbon through the hole to hang the suncatcher in a window.
- Mail the suncatchers to the church shut-ins. Or, give to the visitation pastor so he/she can give the suncatchers to the shut-ins.

Take It Another Step

Allow children to make additional suncatchers for church staff.

Starting a Project

Planning the Program

Goal: To encourage children to plan and help lead an upcoming class or special event. By beginning a project (but not finishing it), you also are adding built-in anticipation for the next class time.

What Do I Need?

- Paper
- Pencil

How Do I Do It?

- Tell the children that planning a class is a big responsibility and that you would like their help in planning and leading a class.
- Choose an upcoming class and lead children in brainstorming activities for the class. You may want to follow a typical class schedule, or you may want to plan a special event for the class. (For a special event, choose the class time closest to Christmas, Valentine's Day or another holiday.) As activities are brainstormed, guide children to make a list of what needs to be done. Ask questions such as:
  - What is the purpose of the meeting (or special event)?
  - How can we accomplish that purpose? (If our purpose is to get more kids to come to our class or club, then we need to figure out how to invite more kids. If our purpose is to learn more about the people who lived back in Bible times, then we need to think of ways we can do that. If our purpose is to help supply a soup kitchen, we need to think of ways to get people to donate food.)
  - Do we want to decorate our room for the occasion? How can we do that?
  - What songs should we sing? Who can accompany us? (Piano? Guitar? Keyboard?)
  - What games should we play?

- Who should pray? What should our prayer focus be?
- What should the lesson or Bible study be about?
- How do we make new kids feel welcome?
- What rules should we make? (Listing rules is only needed for a special event that will meet somewhere other than your usual space.)
- What announcements do we need to make?
- Which children will be responsible for which parts?

As children suggest ideas, listen to what they say. You may get some ideas for additional classes or special events. As the time gets closer for the actual class or special event to happen, meet with the children again to make sure they're prepared. (Note: Keep your expectations of children's responsibilities realistic.)

Take It Another Step

Invite interested children to meet outside of class to do limited planning for classes and/or special events.

Starting a Project
Publishing a Newspaper

Goal: To encourage children to publish a newspaper. By beginning a project (but not finishing it), you also are adding built-in anticipation for the next class time.

What Do I Need?

- Paper
- Pencil
- Markers (for your masthead illustrator)
- Optional—computer

How Do I Do It?

- Lead children to brainstorm and then decide what kind of newspaper they want to produce (see options below). (If a computer is available, an older child with computer skills can take turns entering the information on the computer as others plan.)
    1. A class newspaper focuses on the news of the class and what you've been learning. (This would be the type of newspaper you decide to do each month or quarter.)
    2. A church events newspaper that the children give to parents, staff members and other interested people focuses on church events. (Optional: Produce monthly or quarterly editions and make this an ongoing project to work on when you have time.)
    3. A Bible-times newspaper focuses on a particular time in biblical history. Children might need more time to gather information for this newspaper, but this could be fun and a great learning experience. Consider making the newspaper a year-long project (using extra minutes here and there) since the news would not "get old."
- Design the paper as if it were printed when Noah was building the ark.
- Design the paper as if it were printed when the plagues happened in Egypt. (The children could tell this story from both the Israelite and the Egyptian points of view.)
- Design the paper as if it were printed the day after Christ was born in Bethlehem.
- Decide on a name for the paper. (If you just have five or ten extra minutes, this decision alone could fill the time. Children love to name things.)
- Once you agree on a title, assign your more artistic children to illustrate a masthead (see samples on p. 168).
- List articles and sections you want in your newspaper and how many pages the newspaper will be. (A 2- to 4-page newspaper is a good start.)
    - News
    - Jokes
    - Favorite Bible verses
    - Weather
    - Announcements
    - Comic strips
    - Ads

- Assign each child or pair of children to write a specific section. Have adults ready to assist. If you don't have enough adults, ask older, capable children to serve as helpers.
- Have a teacher or a computer-savvy child enter the text into the computer and set it up as a newspaper. (This will probably need to take place at home during the week.)
- Make copies and distribute to your "audience."

BIBLE-TIMES NEWS PRESS

CLASS BULLETIN

FIRST CHURCH NEWS

Take It Another Step

Start a regular monthly or quarterly newspaper.

Starting a Project
Writing a Song

Goal: To encourage children to write music. By beginning a project (but not finishing it), you also are adding built-in anticipation for the next class time.

What Do I Need?

- Paper
- Pencil

How Do I Do It?

- Help children write a song together by suggesting topics:
  - A theme song for your class, group or club
  - A praise song about God (suggest that children look through the Psalms for ideas)
  - A song about one of God's commands: Ephesians 6:1—obey parents; Ephesians 4:32—be kind; Philippians 2:4—care about the needs of others
  - A song about a Bible character: Gideon, Joshua, David, Daniel, Paul and Silas
- Choose a song that is in the public domain such as "Row, Row, Row Your Boat" or "Jesus Loves Me." Check on the Internet to see if a song is in the public domain, especially if you're planning on publishing the music, even in a church newsletter. (Optional: If you have children in your group who are musical, one or two may be able to compose the music for your song.)
- If children can't get started on their lyrics, suggest some first lines.

> You're the One who created colors—
> the yellow of the sunshine . . . .
>
> The Bible says we must obey
> our dads and moms and what they say.
>
> Paul and Silas preached God's Word,
> But the people didn't want to hear.

Take It Another Step

Include the finished piece in your list of regular songs you sing in class. If the song is outstandingly good, ask the music or worship leader in your church if the children could sing it for the congregation during a worship service or at a church family event.

Starting a Project
Making a Banner

Goal: To encourage children's artistic expression and provide a tool to display a class Bible verse or motto in a prominent place as a reminder.

What Do I Need?

- Bible
- Scratch paper
- Pencil
- Large length of fabric or paper
- Construction paper in a variety of colors
- Various colors and sizes of felt pieces
- Scissors
- Glue
- Optional—shape, object or letter stencils

How Do I Do It?

- Help children choose a Bible verse or phrase, or a class motto.
- Lead children to brainstorm pictures to show on the banner (flowers around the border, arrows, a kitten, etc.).

- As you lead children in planning the banner, sketch it out on scratch paper so everyone will be able to visualize the finished banner.
- Assign each child or pair of children a specific task for the banner.
- Write and cut out letters from paper or felt. (Optional: Children trace around letter stencils.)
- Assign other children to draw on construction paper the flowers, faces, animals, or decorative shapes for the banner. (Optional: Children trace around shape or object stencils.)
- Glue completed letters and illustrations onto banner.

Take It Another Step

Provide a permanent worktable with the banner supplies always available. Children can work on the banner each week when they first come to class and are waiting for others to arrive.

Starting a Project
Teachers Talking

Goal: To give teachers an opportunity to share their own life stories with children.

What Do I Need?

- No supplies needed for this activity (unless you decide to ask teachers to be prepared beforehand)

How Do I Do It?

- Ask teachers to briefly talk to the class, sharing a little of their background and how they came to know Christ as Savior. Remember, the information given needs to be age appropriate. Focus on life-experiences to which a child can relate.
- You may also choose to interview teachers. Here are some sample questions:
  - Did you attend church as a child? When and where?
  - Did you belong to a class or club like this one? When and where?
  - When did you trust Christ as Savior?
  - What were the circumstances? What made you decide to respond to Christ's love and accept His forgiveness?
  - What is your favorite Bible verse? Why?
  - Who is your favorite Bible character? Why?
  - Why are you a teacher at our church?
  - Why did you decide to become a children's pastor, missionary, etc. (for those who work fulltime at the church)?
  - What advice do you have for the children sitting in front of you?
  - What do you want these children to learn about God's Word?
  - How has knowing God's Word helped you in a difficult time? (Tell only age-appropriate stories.)

Take It Another Step

At the beginning of the year, ask teachers to be ready to tell about themselves. Encourage them to bring pictures and a few other childhood mementos. Keep these items in envelopes or boxes in a safe place until you have the necessary free time.

Starting a Project
Talent Show

Goal: To give children an opportunity to display their talents.

What Do I Need?

- No supplies needed for this activity

How Do I Do It?

One of the best ways to keep children and youth interested in the church is to help them feel as if they are part of the church family. Inviting them to participate is a key tool in conveying that feeling.

- Tell your children you are having an instant talent show. Talk about the importance of getting up in front of people and confidently performing. Children (especially older elementary children) tend to dissolve in giggles. Use this as an opportunity to teach the "etiquette" of presentation. Remind them that whatever they do, they are doing it for the Lord. Let children know that their performances do not need to be perfect, but they should do their best.
- Invite any child to sing a song, quote a Bible verse, tell a joke, tell a Bible story, act out a Bible story, quote a poem, do a physical stunt, etc. Encourage the group to listen and watch quietly and respectfully as children perform. (This is not a TV reality show where people make rude comments about someone's talent.)

Take It Another Step

If a child displays an unusually good talent that could be used some way in the adult church service, tell your pastor, children's pastor or music/worship leader.

Starting a Project
Answer the Questions

Goal: To give children an opportunity to ask questions about the Bible.

What Do I Need?

- Bible
- Paper
- Pencil
- Box or other container
- Bible dictionary and/or concordance

How Do I Do It?

- Ask the children to write down their biggest questions about the Bible.
- Put the questions in a box or other container. Pull out and read aloud one question. Answer it on the spot. If you don't know the answer, tell the children you'll check on it during the week and get back to them. If you don't feel confident answering questions by yourself, have all the teachers answer the questions together. Sometimes one teacher knows about one thing and another teacher is more knowledgeable about another subject. Answering the questions together will keep any one teacher from feeling overwhelmed.
- Give the remaining questions (those you don't have time to answer) to a knowledgeable teacher to prepare answers. When you have extra time in the future, answer one or more of the questions.

Take It Another Step

Provide a "suggestion box," paper and a pencil. Keep these items in a visible place in your classroom. Tell children they can submit questions at any time.

Starting a Project
Child on the Spot

Goal: To give children an opportunity to display their knowledge of the Bible.

What Do I Need?
- Bibles
- Real or pretend microphone

How Do I Do It?
- Name a Bible event or a Bible character. Ask for a volunteer to come up and answer questions about the event or character. Then invite other children in the group to ask questions about the event or character. If the child is unable to answer, be ready to supply information or help children find information in the Bible.

Take It Another Step
Have children pretend they are in a TV news show. Videotape children asking questions and the child who answers.

Writing a Commercial

Goal: To give children an opportunity to display their creative talents, and develop some publicity for a church program or event.

What Do I Need?

- Information about an upcoming church program or event
- Markers
- Paper
- Pencils
- Video recorder

How Do I Do It?

- Choose an upcoming event in your church's children's ministry program or in the church itself. Or, select an ongoing church ministry or program.
- Lead children to work together to plan and practice a commercial announcing the event. (If you have a large amount of children, divide into small groups and assign an adult helper to each group. Groups prepare a commercial about the same event, or assign each group a different event.) Children can create an advertising jingle or a skit about the event. Remind children to include information about the event (date, time, cost, location, etc.).
- Allow time for children to practice their commercials.
- Videotape the commercials. (Optional: Show commercials to other groups in the church as appropriate.)

Take It Another Step

With the children's help, create a slogan and appropriate illustration for the children's ministry at your church. Use it in your children's ministry publicity.

Starting a Project
Drawing a Wall Mural

Goal: To give children an opportunity to display their creative talents and learn about the Bible at the same time.

What Do I Need?

- Bible
- Markers or crayons
- Large sheets of construction paper or a large roll of butcher paper
- Tape
- Optional—Bible story pictures

How Do I Do It?

- Lead children to make a wrap-around-the-room mural. If you have a large amount of children, divide into small groups. (If you are using butcher paper, draw lines to divide paper into sections.)
- Give each child or small group one or more sheets of construction paper or assign child or group a section of the butcher paper. Assign the first child or small group the subject of creation, the next Adam and Eve, the next Cain and Abel and so on. The child (or group) draws a picture of that particular Bible event or character. (Optional: Provide Bible story pictures as reference.)
- Hang the pictures in order on the wall, overlapping them slightly so you have a continuous timeline, or attach butcher paper to wall.

Options

Instead of a chronological look at the Bible, children make a mural showing events in one of the following:

- The Israelites' journey in the wilderness (a picture on each of the plagues, the crossing of the Red Sea, etc.)
- The life of David
- The life of Joshua
- Paul's missionary journeys

Take It Another Step

Choose a child with good handwriting and ask him or her to print captions or appropriate Scripture references for each picture in the mural. Provide Bible concordances for children to use in finding references.

177

Nothing is better than a good story and stories are a valuable filler activity. You don't have to run to the church office and copy papers or set up the room in a specific way. As soon as you face a teaching emergency, you can start right in. Children don't have the opportunity to get restless. Tell the story well the first time and children may ask for it a second or third time.

Keeping a couple stories in your "brain file," is good for another reason. Not all "what-can-I-do-with-the-kids" moments are in your classroom. Maybe your class of third graders is on the church steps waiting restlessly for a bus to take them to a children's concert. Or maybe your class is stuck in a tiny pavilion during a rain-soaked picnic. Have a couple of stories in your mind so when those well-planned moments suddenly become unplanned moments, you are ready to go.

You can also use the stories on pages 179-187 as read-aloud times for the children in your classes. The tips below will help you make stories whether told or read aloud an engaging activity for children.

Telling the Story

Ten Tips for Storytelling

1. Stand so your back is against a blank wall. Windows, doorways and pictures can easily distract children.
2. Categorize the stories for the children. Children need to know when a story is from the Bible and that, therefore, the story is true. They need to know that the funny story about purple snow is made up. (Instead of saying Bible "stories," you might want to consider using Bible "adventures" or Bible "events." This takes the fictional "story" aspect out of what you are saying and is another step in helping young children understand the difference between truth and fiction.)

   There are three types of stories:
   - From the Bible: This adventure is from the Bible and therefore true. (Explain that parables were stories Jesus told.)
   - From personal experience: This story is true. It really happened, but it is NOT from the Bible.
   - From your imagination (or someone else's imagination): This story is NOT true. I made it up (or read it in a book, etc.).
3. Know the story well, but don't hesitate to use your own words.
4. Start right in with the story. Other than saying, "This is from the Bible," or "I wrote this story for you," don't give a long introduction.
5. Get your audience's attention with an exciting first sentence. Don't start by telling children to "listen up" or "quiet down." Start with a loud voice or a whisper. Both will get the children's interest. Use a lot of expression. Shout, scream and pretend to cry. Look happy, sad or afraid. Throw yourself into it. You'll keep their attention.
6. Walk around as you talk.
7. Use eye contact. Look at each child individually. If a child is restless, don't stop the story, but walk over and talk right at him for a few seconds. Usually the child will quiet.
8. Memorize the first line and the last line. You'll need to get off to a good start and you'll need a tight finish.
9. Recognize that all age groups enjoy a well-told story (even adults).
10. Enjoy the telling, and your audience will enjoy the listening

Telling the Story
Telling a Bible Adventure

Goal: To tell the children a true Bible event that will both entertain and teach.

What Do I Need?

- Bible

How Do I Do It?

- Tell the story with enthusiasm!
- Ask some of the discussion questions at the end of the story.

Not a Happy-Ever-After Story

Do you like to hear adventures about princesses and kings? I want to tell you about a REAL princess and a REAL king who lived a long, long time ago. I know this adventure is true because I read about it in the Bible. Right here in 2 Chronicles 22. (Point to your open Bible.)

But I will need YOUR help.

Boys, every time I point at you I want you to sadly shake your head "no" and say "What was HE thinking?" Sometimes you'll have to say "What was SHE thinking?" You need to say it as if you can't believe that the person made such a bad choice. Can you do that for me now? (Have the boys repeat "What was HE thinking?" two or three times.) Good.

Girls, every time I point at you I want you to say "Shhh." Can you do that for me now? (Have the girls say "shhh" a few times.)

Great! We're all set to go.

(Open with prayer and as soon as you say "Amen" start the story.)

Once upon a time, a long, long time ago, there lived a princess named Jehosheba. Now Jehosheba might have lived in the palace, but that wasn't always the best place to live. Oh, no!

Jehosheba grew up to be a young women who obeyed God. She married a high priest named Jehoiada. (A high priest was one of the men who was in charge of the Temple of the TRUE God.)

But things just got worse in the kingdom of Judah. Jehosheba's dad, Jehoram, didn't care anything about God. He was so mean, he had all his brothers killed so they couldn't be the next king.

(Point to the boys. What WAS he thinking?)

Lots of fighting was going on and all Jehosheba's older brothers were killed in the war. Then her father got a stomach disease and he died, too. Sadly, no one cared about him because he had been such a bad king. He wasn't even buried in the kingly tomb!

For awhile Ahaziah, the youngest son was king, but Athaliah (his wicked stepmother) saw this as her BIG chance. She would get rid of ALL Jehoram's grandsons. When Ahaziah died, SHE WOULD BE THE QUEEN!

179

(Boys, this time you need to say, "What was SHE thinking?" Point to the boys. What WAS she thinking?)

(Whisper this part suspensefully.) Jehosheba heard about this wicked plan and she came up with a plan of her own. With her husband, Jehoiada, they would take the baby grandson, Joash, and hide him in the bedroom of the palace.

(Point to the girls. Shhh.)

Hiding the baby took a lot of courage. (Don't you think if Athaliah knew that Jehosheba had hidden the baby, she would've gotten rid of Jehosheba and her husband, too? Sure, she would have.) Athaliah THOUGHT she had gotten rid of all the boys who were in line to be king, but she didn't know about, or just forgot about little Joash.

(Point to the girls. Shhh.)

Athaliah was SO happy! Now she had the kingdom to herself. She destroyed part of the Temple built to honor the true God to get stuff to build a temple to honor one of the false gods, Baal.

(Point to the boys. What WAS she thinking?)

After awhile, Jehosheba and her husband, Jehoiada decided to take the baby to live at the Temple where they worshiped the true God. After all, Athaliah certainly wouldn't be at the temple to worship God! That would be the best place of all to hide him.

(Point to the girls. Shhh.)

For six years, the wicked queen Athaliah ruled Judah. The people didn't like her. They wanted their rightful king, someone who was in the line (family) of David. For six years the wicked queen Athaliah led her kingdom in worshipping Baal.

(Point to the girls. Shhh.)

During this time, however, Jehoiada and Jehosheba quietly taught Joash about the true God. They taught him to love the God who had brought the people out of Egypt and to the Promised Land. They taught him that God loved him, too.

But after a while, the people of Judah were getting restless. Jehoiada decided it was time to let them know about Joash.

Jehoiada waited until Athaliah was busy ruling the people and then he called for men from all over Judah to come to the Temple. Crowds of people came to see what was happening.

Jehoiada brought out Joash and introduced him—the seven-year-old rightful king!

Oh, the people were excited as the high priest and his sons anointed Joash king and put a crown on his head. They all shouted, "Long live the king!"

Athaliah heard the people cheering and ran to the Temple, wondering what was happening, and there was the new king, the rightful king.

And that was the end of the rule of Athaliah, the wicked stepmother.

As Joash grew, his uncle Jehoiada helped him rule the people and when he became a man he led the kingdom in worshipping the true God.

One of the most important things he did was make the Temple look new again. All because his Aunt Jehosheba and Uncle Jehoiada loved God and did a very brave thing in hiding baby Joash.

God cared about Joash. He protected him against the wicked queen.

He gave him an aunt and uncle who loved God and cared about him.

Sadly, however, this palace story of kings and queens doesn't have a happy ending.

Sadly, once Jehoiada died, Joash began listening to the people who worshipped idols and did some things that were not pleasing to God.

He listened to the wrong people and he forgot about God's love.

(Point to the boys. What WAS he thinking?)

We forget, too, don't we?

God has done so much for us. He created us. He loves us. He sent His Son, the Lord Jesus Christ, to die for our sins. He came alive again and is living in heaven, preparing a place for us to live.

Like Joash, we sometimes listen to what other people tell us to do and we forget about what God tells us to do.

The story of Joash is a good one to remember. His uncle and aunt needed a lot of courage to hide him for six years. They taught him well.

But he chose to forget God and because of that God allowed him to lose his kingdom.

How sad.

The next time a friend is trying to get you to do something you shouldn't do, remember Princess Jehosheba and the King Joash. One listened to God and did the right thing. The other made a wrong choice and lost an entire kingdom.

(Pray, asking God for wisdom for the children to make good choices in their lives.)

Ask:

1. Some of the kings worshipped the true God, but many worshipped idols. What are the differences between God and an idol? (God is alive, an idol is made out of stone. An idol can't hear you pray. An idol can't do anything.)
2. Why do you think Jehosheba hid Joash? (Because she loved God, she understood what a wicked thing her stepmother was doing in getting rid of everyone in the family. She saw the opportunity to save the baby and she did so.)
3. Why do you think Joash turned away from God after everything he had been taught and had done? (He listened to other people. Peer pressure.)
4. What do people do today that isn't any different from Joash? (They go to church on Sunday and then on Monday do whatever they want or allow someone to lead them into doing something that is wrong.)

Take It Another Step

Explain how Joash was in the line (family) of David. If he had died, David's line (family) would have stopped. Yet, it had been prophesied that the Messiah would come from David's family. God was truly at work here with this godly princess and her brave husband.

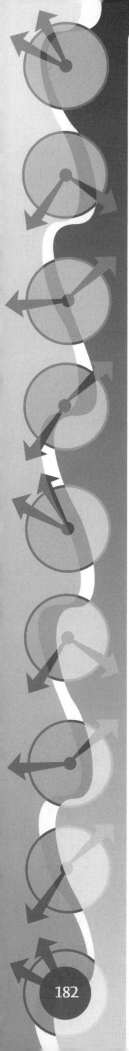

Telling the Story
The Personal Experience

Goal: To share an interesting personal experience story that teaches ways to love and obey God.

What Do I Need?

- No supplies needed for this activity

How Do I Do It?

- Personal experience stories are great! They're already in your "brain bank" ready for the telling and you don't get mixed up about what comes next.
- Children love to hear about your childhood experiences. Often teachers say, "My life wasn't all that interesting. I wouldn't have any personal experiences to share." However, it is the little, everyday moments that can often be expanded to an attention-getting story for children.
- Some things to remember about sharing personal experiences:
  1. Choose an experience that is appropriate for sharing with children. Choices should be subjects such as a new pet, your family vacation or winning the swimming trophy. Stay away from adult topics.
  2. Stick to the subject. If you are telling the story of the day your mom had triplets, don't stumble around attempting to remember the name of the hospital, the doctor and the exact time they were born. (Sometimes we tend to go on and on when talking about ourselves.)
  3. Relate how the Lord used the experience in your own life or use the experience to paint a word picture of a spiritual truth. You may think this would be difficult, but it really isn't.
- Here are some examples from my own life and how I've used them to teach.
  1. Laughing about someone's mother without realizing that her daughter was in the group listening to me. (I shouldn't have been laughing even if the daughter WASN'T there.) Life Application: Always watching what we say and making sure our words are kind. (See Colossians 4:6; Ecclesiastes 10:12.)
  2. Being frightened because I thought someone was breaking into our house when I was watching my younger brother. And yes, there WAS someone on the back porch, but it was someone we knew. The story has a funny ending, so it is not an overall scary story. Life Application: Trusting in the Lord. Asking the Lord for courage in tough situations. (See Hebrews 13:6, Psalm 56:3.)
  3. Overhearing one girl ask another girl for the answer to a test question and understanding they were cheating—and also knowing that the shared answer was incorrect. Life Application: Being honest in all situations. A good example of the premise: "Be sure your sin will find you out"—because they both were marked wrong. (See Philippians 4:8; Numbers 32:23.)
- Try it the next time *you* have an unexpected 10 minutes to fill.
  1. Your story about an unusual pet.
     Life Application: God's wonderful creation. (See Genesis 1:1; Psalm 148.)

2. Your story about lying.
   Life Application: Speaking the truth. (See Colossians 1:9.)
3. Your story about making a new friend.
   Life Application: The importance of friendship. (See Proverbs 17:17.)
4. Your story about having a good time with a grandparent.
   Life Application: Loving your grandparents. (See Proverbs 17:6.)
5. Your story about sports.
   Life Application: You did it for a temporary award. As Christians we receive an eternal reward. (See 1 Corinthians 9:24-25.)

Take It Another Step

Give children a subject and asked them to share personal experiences. Subjects should be positive: the day they won an award, the funniest thing that's happened to them, the best place they've visited.

183

Telling the Story
The Fiction Story

Goal: To tell a story that entertains and teaches ways of loving and obeying God.

What Do I Need?

- No supplies needed for this activity

How Do I Do It?

- Fiction stories are fun to tell. They are also good discussion starters. Children will talk about a fictional character more readily than themselves or a friend.
- Here is a story to get you started. The key to this story is to make the Mallory Johnson character be a fast talker. Children love it and you will have no trouble keeping their attention.

At the Corner of Barkley and 57th Street

I met Mallory Johnson on a beginning-of-summer Tuesday. I was sitting in front of my apartment house very busily being bored. Of course, I spend most of my time busily being bored.

My mother says, "Rachel, life is only boring to boring people."

My brother says, "Rachel, when you get to college, you'll probably major in boredom."

My father says, "Rachel, God created a wonderful world for us to enjoy. It's a sin to be bored."

The way I see it, if I lived someplace exotic like Abu Dhabi or Japan, then I wouldn't be bored. Or if I lived in the country with horses to ride and trees to climb, I wouldn't be bored. But where do I live? Right here at the corner of Barkley and 57th Street and there's not a tree in sight.

Well, I take that back. We live across the street from Sunshine Acres Nursing Home and they DO have a scrawny little pine tree out front. Actually, I don't get the Sunshine Acres thing. First of all, where are the acres? They have exactly one city lot, that's it. And where is the sunshine? Unless you're standing in the middle of the street in the middle of the day when the sun happens to be straight up in the sky, the buildings block the sun.

So, anyhow, I was sitting on the front step being bored when suddenly this girl about my own age comes in stands in front of me. I haven't seen her before and I know I've seen everyone who lives on my block. She stares at me.

I stare back.

(Remember, Mallory talks a mile a minute and hardly takes a breath. You need to talk fast. Keep going with Mallory's introduction speech as long as you can. Children will enjoy listening to you "speed talk.")

Then suddenly she says: "Hi, my name is Mallory Johnson and I just moved here from Iowa. I didn't want to leave Iowa because all my friends are there and we even had to leave my cat there and

I've lived there all my life, but now that I've met you, I'm glad we've moved because I know we'll be good friends because I think I've seen you before. I know where I've seen you. That was your dad and mom who sang in church Sunday morning, wasn't it? I watched them sit down and I remember thinking that their daughter was the same age I was and that was you and I live right around the corner. My parents said we'll be going to that church. They liked it a lot and what's your name anyhow?"

"Rachel Katzman."

"Oh, Rachel. I love the name Rachel. Anyhow, I didn't want to leave Iowa but now that I've met you, Rachel, I think I will like it here. Maybe later you can go down to that deli on the corner with me. We didn't have delis where I lived in Iowa so I don't know what to order, but Dad and Mom are still busy unpacking, so Mom said I could get lunch there. She gave me enough money that I can buy you lunch, too, if you tell me what is good and all and I was thinking we should go across the street and talk to the lady who is sitting out there in the wheelchair because she looks just like my great-grandma and my great-grandma even has a blue sweater like that but my great-grandma lives in Kansas, so I know it's not her. Let's go see her, OK?"

I didn't know what to say. I had never been across the street to the nursing home before.

"Come on, Rachel, you CAN cross the street, can't you?"

Well, I could. I was allowed to go anywhere as long as my mom could see me out of the apartment window.

So we walked up to the corner, crossed at the light and then walked right up to the front of Sunshine Acres Nursing Home to the lady sitting outside in the wheelchair.

I didn't have any idea what to say to her, but I shouldn't have worried.

(Say as fast as you can.) "Hi, my name is Mallory Johnson and this is my best friend Rachel Katzman. Well, we haven't been best friends for long, only about five minutes, but we're planning on becoming even better friends, aren't we Rachel?" But she didn't stop long enough for me to answer.

"I used to live in Iowa and I didn't want to move because that's where all my friends are and even my cat and I've lived there all my life, but now we live here and I met Rachel so I know everything will be OK. 'Cause Rachel lives right over there and I live in the brick apartment building around the corner. We even go to the same church. We came to see you because you look just like my great-grandmother. My great-grandmother even has a blue sweater like yours, but she lives in Kansas so I know you're not her. What's your name?"

The lady laughed, a bubbly laughed that came from deep inside of her.

(Use a shaky voice for Mrs. Rose.) "Mrs. Rose," she said, still laughing. "And, aren't you something else Mallory Johnson?"

"People tell me that." Mallory shrugged. "How long have you lived here?"

(Shaky voice) "Five years."

"Oh." Mallory's voice turned sad. "That's too bad."

(Shaky voice) "Honey, don't feel sorry for me. My son is a pilot and he's out of town a lot, but soon as he gets in, he comes over and sees me. Some of these people have no one to visit them. That's who I feel sorry for."

Just then a nurse came out to get Mrs. Rose for lunch.

(Shaky voice) "You girls come back and see me," she said as the nurse wheeled her inside.

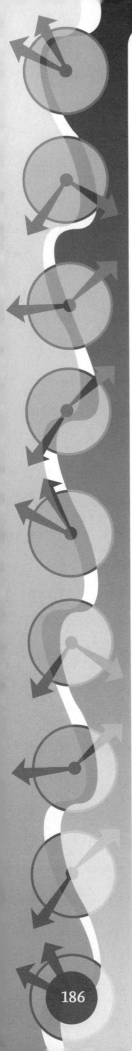

"Oh, we will, we will, won't we Rachel? Now, come on, we can go to the deli and I'll need you to tell me what to get."

Well, that night at the supper table my brother said, "What did you do all day, Rachel? Sit around being bored?"

"No way," I told him and then I explained all about Mallory Johnson and Mrs. Rose and the deli.

The next morning Mallory was sitting on my front step when I went downstairs.

"Where have you been, Rachel? I've been here FOREVER!"

I looked down the street at the clock on the bank. It was 8 o'clock. She couldn't have been there TOO long.

"Come on, Rachel. Mrs. Rose is already outside waiting for us. See?" She pointed across the street.

I looked. Sure enough, there was Mrs. Rose sitting in her wheelchair and when I looked at her, she waved.

"Let's go." Mallory grabbed my hand and pulled me to the end of the street, across at the corner and down the other side.

Mrs. Rose had a big smile on her face. (Shaky voice) "I was hoping you girls would come back. I wanted to show you a picture of my son, Peter." She held up a photo of a man in a pilot's uniform.

"Oh," said Mallory. "He looks so brave!" And we all laughed at the way she said it.

Mrs. Rose put the picture back in her pocket. (Shaky voice) "Now, girls tell me all about your church."

(Say as fast as you can.) "I can't tell you much about it." Mallory looked at me. "But Rachel can. I think she's probably been going to that church for a long time, haven't you. Rachel? And I hope our family will be going there for a long time, too. But Rachel will have to tell you about the church."

"Well . . . ," I hesitated. "Well, it's a good church. Our pastor teaches us about the Bible. And we have a children's choir. At Easter, we did an entire musical. That was fun."

(Shaky voice) "Oh, to hear children sing again." Mrs. Rose looked sort of dreamy-eyed. "We used to have a preacher come here to the nursing home every Sunday afternoon. Sometimes he would bring the children from his church to sing for us, but when he moved no one from the church ever came back again. I would so enjoy hearing children sing."

"So," said Mallory, "sing for her, Rachel!"

"Here?"

"Sure."

"What should I sing?"

"Sing one of those songs from the Easter musical."

So right there on the corner of Barkley and 57th Street, I sang a solo. When I was done, Mrs. Rose, Mallory and some people walking by on the street, applauded.

I felt kind of silly with everyone looking at me.

(Shaky voice) "That was wonderful." Mrs. Rose patted my hand.

"You were awesome!" Mallory clapped some more.

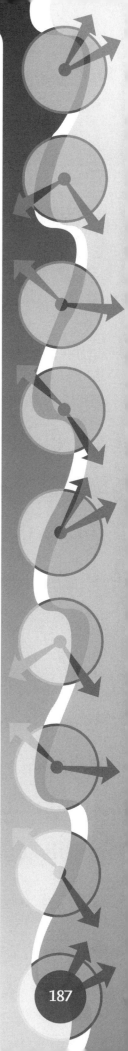

"Sounds better with the parts," I said.

Mallory's face brightened. (Say as fast as you can.) "So bring the parts. Bring all the kids. You think your choir director would do that? Mrs. Rose just said she would like to hear children sing again and that other church doesn't come anymore. Maybe our church could come or at least the kids from our church could come. Could you ask, Rachel? Please."

"Yes, I could ask." Inside I was getting excited. Maybe our choir COULD sing at Sunshine Acres.

I waited until right before supper to call Mr. Keith on Dad's cell phone and I told him about Mallory and Mrs. Rose and the solo I sang on the sidewalk. "Do you think we could do the musical?" I asked.

"I think we could work that out, Rachel. You kids could sing and I could give a short devotional. Yes, I think it would work. I'll give the manager of the nursing home a call."

I was still listening to Mr. Keith as I ran (with the phone) down the stairs of our apartment building, around the corner to Mallory's apartment building and up the stairs to her apartment. Fortunately, Mr. Keith hung up because I was totally out of breath.

I only had to knock on the door once before Mallory flung it open.

"He said 'yes!' I told her.

Mallory jumped up and down. (Say as fast as you can.) "That is SO WONDERFUL. I was thinking my mom could make cookies and your mom could make cookies and we could get some other ladies in the church to make cookies and we could buy some rolls of crepe paper because crepe paper doesn't cost that much and we could have a party—a real party! Wouldn't Mrs. Rose and her friends love a party? You know I didn't want to move from Iowa and leave all my friends back there and all, but now I'm glad I moved because I met you, Rachel. and I think living at the corner of Barkley and 57th Street is the very best place in the whole world to live."

You know, someday I still would like to live somewhere exotic like Abu Dhabi or Japan or in the country with horses to ride and trees to climb.

But for right now?

I agree with Mallory that living at the corner of Barkley and 57th Street is the very best place in the entire world to live.

Ask:

1. What was Rachel's problem before Mallory moved to town? (She was always bored.)
2. What kind of person was Mallory? (Someone who could find something exciting about anything. Someone who was kind to other people—kids her own age and the people at the nursing home. She knew how to be content.)
3. What advice does the Bible give fits this situation? (Ephesians 4:32—be kind; Philippians 4:12—being content wherever you are.)

Take It Another Step

Write a story as a class. Make sure it includes a life application of Bible truth. Children illustrate the story. Print it out on the computer.

187

Thinking About the Bible

Fun Facts

Goal: To teach children facts about the Bible in a fun way. Many children think knowing unusual facts are a lot of fun, and they like to impress others with their knowledge.

What Do I Need?

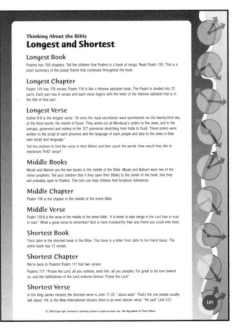

- Bible for each child or group of children
- A copy of either page 189, 190 or pages 191-194

How Do I Do It?

- Ask children if they know the facts on the page you selected ("Which is the longest book in the Bible?") Some children may know the more obvious answers, but guessing is fine. After three or four incorrect guesses, tell them the correct answer and have them find the verse, chapter or book in the Bible. Talk with children about the answers, using the information provided on the pages.

Take It Another Step

Invite children to make a series of Bible trivia cards. Children write a question on the front of an index card and an answer on the back. Keep the cards handy for quick trivia games.

Thinking About the Bible
Longest and Shortest

Longest Book

Psalms has 150 chapters. Tell the children that Psalms is a book of songs. Read Psalm 150. This is a short summary of the praise theme that continues throughout the book.

Longest Chapter

Psalm 119 has 176 verses. Psalm 119 is like a Hebrew alphabet book. The Psalm is divided into 22 parts. Each part has 8 verses and each verse begins with the letter of the Hebrew alphabet that is in the title of that part.

Longest Verse

Esther 8:9 is the longest verse: "At once the royal secretaries were summoned—on the twenty-third day of the third month, the month of Sivan. They wrote out all Mordecai's orders to the Jews, and to the satraps, governors and nobles of the 127 provinces stretching from India to Cush. These orders were written in the script of each province and the language of each people and also to the Jews in their own script and language."

Tell the children to find the verse in their Bibles and then count the words. How would they like to memorize THAT verse?

Middle Books

Micah and Nahum are the two books in the middle of the Bible. Micah and Nahum were two of the minor prophets. Tell your children that if they open their Bibles to the center of the book, that they will probably open to Psalms. This hint can help children find Scripture references.

Middle Chapter

Psalm 118 is the chapter in the middle of the entire Bible.

Middle Verse

Psalm 118:8 is the verse in the middle of the entire Bible: "It is better to take refuge in the Lord than to trust in man." What a great verse to remember! God is more trustworthy than any friend you could ever have.

Shortest Book

Third John is the shortest book in the Bible. This book is a letter from John to his friend Gaius. The entire book has 13 verses.

Shortest Chapter

We're back to Psalms! Psalm 117 has two verses.

Psalms 117: "Praise the Lord, all you nations; extol him, all you peoples. For great is his love toward us, and the faithfulness of the Lord endures forever. Praise the Lord."

Shortest Verse

In the *King James Version*, the shortest verse is John 11:35: "Jesus wept." That's the one people usually talk about. Yet, in the *New International Version,* there is an even shorter verse: "He said" (Job 3:2).

Thinking About the Bible
Words

Longest Word in the Bible

Maher-shalal-hash-baz is the longest word in the Bible (see Isaiah 8:1). It is the name given to Isaiah's son. The name means "spoil hastens, prey speeds."

First and Last Word in the Bible

"In" is the first word in the Bible (see Genesis 1:1—"In the beginning God created the heavens and the earth.").

"Amen" is the last word in the Bible (see Revelation 22:21—"The grace of the Lord Jesus be with God's people. Amen.").

Greek Alphabet

Have you heard someone quote Revelation 22:13—"I am the Alpha and the Omega, the First and the Last, the Beginning and the End."? (Or maybe you've memorized the verse yourself.) Did you ever wonder what Alpha and Omega were?

Alpha is the first letter of the Greek alphabet and Omega is the last letter. They are used to show that God is the beginning and ending of everything and all things in between.

A Book All About God Without Using the Word "God"

Esther is a great book about a daring royal adventure. Esther makes courageous (and dangerous) choices and God uses her courage to save His people. Esther is truly a record of God watching out for the Israelites, yet the book of Esther does not mention the name of God even once.

Word Pictures

God uses word pictures to describe His Word. Here are five of them.

- A sword. Ephesians 6:17—"Take the helmet of salvation and the sword of the Spirit, which is the word of God."
- Milk. 1 Peter 2:2—"Like newborn babies, crave pure spiritual milk, so that by it you may grow up in your salvation."
- Honey. Psalm 119:103—"How sweet are your words to my taste, sweeter than honey to my mouth!"
- Bread. Matthew 4:4—"Jesus answered, 'It is written: Man does not live on bread alone, but on every word that comes from the mouth of God.'"
- Light. Psalm 119:105—"Your word is a lamp to my feet and a light for my path."

Thinking About the Bible
Did You Know?

Did You Know That There's a Verse in the Bible That Tells You Not to Study Too Hard?

Ecclesiastes 12:12—"Be warned, my son, of anything in addition to them. Of making many books there is no end, and much study wearies the body."

Sorry, that doesn't mean you shouldn't do your best at school. What the verse does mean is people (usually adults, not kids) sometimes go after more and more education, not putting what they've learned to use. Or they gain lots of knowledge, but don't use what they've learned in a wise way.

The verse also means a person shouldn't look for answers to the hard questions of life in books that don't talk about God.

So, you could try quoting the verse to your parents the next time you want to get out of homework—but maybe you better not!

Did You Know There's a King in the Bible Who Got into a Lot of Trouble for Pointing?

A prophet of God told Jeroboam that God would destroy his altars and that made Jeroboam angry. He pointed at the prophet and commanded his men to "Grab him!"

Guess what? His hand just withered up right there while he was pointing to the prophet. Well, if that wasn't enough to make the king have a bad day, his altar split open and all the ashes poured out.

Suddenly (hmmm . . .) King Jeroboam believed in God and asked the prophet to heal his hand.

Which he did.

So, the king said, "Come home and I'll feed you supper and give you a gift, but the prophet said no, and left town." (See 1 Kings 3:1-10.)

Did You Know There's a Verse in the *King James Version* of the Bible That Talks About the Pilots Making Noise in the Suburbs?

Ezekiel 27:28—"The suburbs shall shake at the sound of the cry of thy pilots."

That's kind of funny because planes make lots of noise in the suburbs every day!

The pilots in this verse, however, were captains of ships. Suburbs, like now, meant cities.

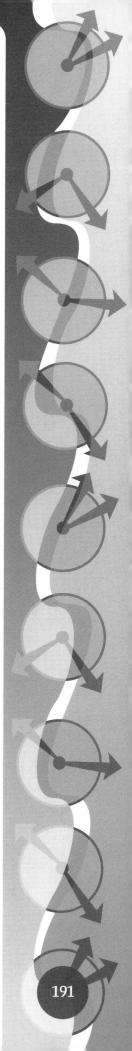

191

Did You Know That King Xerxes (The Husband of Esther) Gave a Party for His Nobles and Officials That Lasted Six Months?

What DO you do at a six-month-long party? Then, when he was done with the party, he had a seven day feast. OK, even if you were really, really, really hungry, could you eat for seven days straight? (See Esther 1:1-5.)

Did You Know Belshazzar Had a Banquet for 1,000 of His Nobles?

This banquet turned out to be quite a party!

Everyone was sitting around drinking and having a great time when Belshazzar got an idea—why not get all the gold goblets that had been taken from the temple of God in Jerusalem and hand them out so the party-goers could drink from them?

So they did and sat around and praised all the gold, silver and bronze idols and were having a happy time.

Suddenly, however, the fingers of a human hand started writing on the wall. Now, THAT would be a party stopper. In fact, King Belshazzar grew so frightened, that his knees started knocking and his legs gave way underneath him.

He called everyone he could think of to interpret what the hand was writing, but only Daniel could do the job.

This is what the words said: MENE, MENE, TEKEL, PARSIN.

This is what the words meant:

Mene: God has numbered the days of your reign and brought it to an end.

Tekel: You have been weighed on the scales and found wanting.

Peres: Your kingdom is divided and given to the Medes and Persians.

That was the END of THAT party. (See Daniel 5.)

By the way, some people think that's where the expression "I saw the handwriting on the wall" came from.

Did You Know That There's a National Park in Israel Called Harod Spring?

That's the site where Gideon camped with his army. (Remember when God told him he needed to get rid of some men?) The park has a swimming pool and beautiful, flowering trees. (If you have a computer in your classroom, look on the Internet to see pictures of the park.) (See Judges 7:1.)

Did You Know There's a Verse in the Bible That Says Sort of the Same Thing Your Mom Says Before You Go to a Birthday Party?

Your mom says: "Don't eat too much sugar, you'll get sick." God's way of saying it is: Proverbs 25:16—"If you find honey, eat just enough—too much of it, and you will vomit."

Did You Know That Esau Got in BIG Trouble for Eating a Bowl of Stew?

Did YOU ever say, "I'm starving to death?" Esau came in from the fields and smelled the delicious stew his brother was cooking. "Quick, give me some," he begged, "I'm starving to death."

Jacob said he would if Esau would give him his birthright.

What a foolish trade! For a bowl of stew, Esau gave away all the rights he had as a firstborn child. (See Genesis 25:29–26:1.)

Did You Know That Red Sky at Night Is a Sailor's Delight and Red Sky in Morning Is a Sailor's Warning?

Have you ever heard your dad or mom say those words? These words come RIGHT from the Bible. Matthew 16:2-3—"He replied, 'When evening comes, you say, "It will be fair weather, for the sky is red," and in the morning, "Today it will be stormy, for the sky is red and overcast." You know how to interpret the appearance of the sky, but you cannot interpret the signs of the times.'"

Did You Know That Swaddling a Baby Was Something Done to Many Infants Born at the Time of Christ?

When babies were born, they were washed and rubbed with salt. Then they were wrapped tightly with legs together and arms down at their side. Sometimes five or six yards of linen were used to swaddle the baby with the cloth also wrapped under the baby's chin and across the forehead. Moms thought that swaddling their babies helped them to sleep well and not be so fussy.

Did You Know That the Phrase "Like Mother, Like Daughter" Comes from the Bible?

This phrase is used in Ezekiel 16:44—"Everyone who quotes proverbs will quote this proverb about you: 'Like mother, like daughter.'"

Did You Know That No One Knows What Gopher Wood Is?

Do you sometimes hear people say that Noah's ark was made of gopher wood? Well, Bible scholars (those people who study the Bible ALL the time), don't know what gopher wood is. (See Genesis 6.)

But here are some facts we do know about Noah's Ark.

- Noah's ark was 450 feet (137 m) long, 75 feet (23 m) wide and 45 feet (135 m) high. (If you're meeting during the daytime and have a large church yard or parking lot, walk 450 steps with your class. Children and adults are often surprised at how long Noah's ark really was.
- Noah's ark had three floors.
- Noah's ark had one window and one door.
- You know all those pictures of Noah's ark with the elephant standing on the deck

193

and the giraffe looking out the sunroof? The ark didn't look like that at all. It was a long, flat, rectangular box.

Did You Know Those Frogs in Egypt Didn't Just Disappear?

You remember the 10 plagues, right? The plagues were the calamities Pharaoh had to deal with when he refused to let God's people go? Think about just the plague of frogs for a few minutes.

After God removed the plague, the frogs died and then . . . well, then they were lying all over the place. Everywhere the people looked, there were dead frogs. So they put them in piles and then they stunk. (See Exodus 8:13-14.)

Did You Know the Phrase "Go the Extra Mile" Comes from the Bible?

In Matthew 5:41 Jesus told a crowd of people: "If someone forces you to go one mile, go with him two miles."

Did You Know There Were Probably More Than 3,000,000 Israelites Traveling to the Promised Land?

Have you seen pictures people have drawn of the Exodus? How many people were in the picture? A couple dozen? A couple hundred? In Numbers 1:46, we read that there were 603,550 men and that wasn't even counting the tribe of Levi. That number didn't include the wives or kids either. So the total was probably more than 3,000,000.

Thinking About the Bible
Is It in the Bible?

Goal: For children to have fun and learn about the Bible at the same time. (Most of these quotes will be unfamiliar and children may be surprised that they're in the Bible.)

What Do I Need?

- Copy of Food in the Bible, Animals in the Bible, or Living the Life (pp. 197-199) for each child.
- Pencil
- Small prizes

How Do I Do It?

- Give each child a copy of the page you selected and a pencil. Children check the box marked "in" if they think the quote is from the Bible and "out" if they think the quote is not from the Bible. Winning child (or team if this is a team project) receives a prize. Variation: Read the quotes aloud and discuss as a group whether or not they are from the Bible. Ask the children to look the true verses up in the Bible and read them to the class. (Bible phrases are from the *NIV*.)

Take It Another Step

You could divide the groups into teams and challenge the teams to come up with quotes. Other teams must guess whether or not the quote is from the Bible. Allow teams to use their Bibles.

Answers

Food in the Bible

1. Is there flavor in the white of an egg? (Job 6:6)
2. Prepare me the kind of tasty food I like. (Genesis 27:4)
3. When you have only two pennies left in the world, buy a loaf of bread with one, and a lily with the other. (Chinese Proverb)
4. He looked around, and there by his head was a cake. (1 Kings 19:6)
5. Choose an orange from the orange tree. (From no where!)
6. But the fig tree replied, "Should I give up my fruit, so good and sweet?" (Judges 9:11)
7. His speech is smooth as butter. (Psalm 55:21)
8. Give me neither poverty nor riches, but give me only my daily bread. (Proverbs 30:8)
9. Laughter is brightest, in the place where the food is. (Irish Proverb)
10. The rich worry over their money, the poor over their bread. (Vietnamese Proverb)

Animals in the Bible

1. Whom are you pursuing? A dead dog? A flea? (1 Samuel 24:14)
2. Do horses run on the rocky crags? (Amos 6:12)
3. The reason a dog has so many friends is that he wags his tail instead of his tongue. (Anonymous)

195

4. A bird does not sing because it has an answer. It sings because it has a song. (Chinese Proverb)
5. As the deer pants for streams of water, so my soul pants for you, O God (Psalm 42:1)
6. Even a live dog is better off than a dead lion! (Ecclesiastes 9:4)
7. Go to the ant, you sluggard; consider its ways and be wise! (Proverbs 6:6)
8. Does a wild donkey bray when it has grass, or an ox bellow when it has fodder? (Job 6:5)
9. Like a roaring lion or a charging bear is a wicked man ruling over a helpless people. (Proverbs 28:15)
10. A dog is man's best friend. (Unknown)

Living the Life

1. He laughs at the commotion in the town; he does not hear a driver's shout. (Job 39:7)
2. Eat to live, not live to eat. (Ben Franklin)
3. A righteous man cares for the needs of his animal. (Proverbs 12:10)
4. Early to bed, early to rise, makes a man healthy, wealthy and wise. (Ben Franklin)
5. A gossip betrays a confidence, but a trustworthy man keeps a secret. (Proverbs 11:13)
6. Children are a gift from God; they are his reward. (Psalms 127:3)
7. For the love of money is a root of all kinds of evil. (1 Timothy 6:10)
8. A happy heart makes the face cheerful. (Proverbs 15:13)
9. Lazy hands make a man poor, but diligent hands bring wealth. (Proverbs 10:4)
10. God helps them who help themselves. (Ben Franklin)

Thinking About the Bible
Food in the Bible

Which of the following phrases are in the Bible?

Check the "in" box if you think the phrase is in the Bible. Check the "out" box if you don't think it's in the Bible.

1. Is there flavor in the white of an egg?

   ☐ IN   ☐ OUT

2. Prepare me the kind of tasty food I like.

   ☐ IN   ☐ OUT

3. When you have only two pennies left in the world, buy a loaf of bread with one, and a lily with the other.

   ☐ IN   ☐ OUT

4. He looked around, and there by his head was a cake.

   ☐ IN   ☐ OUT

5. Choose an orange from the orange tree.

   ☐ IN   ☐ OUT

6. But the fig tree replied, "Should I give up my fruit, so good and sweet?"

   ☐ IN   ☐ OUT

7. His speech is smooth as butter.

   ☐ IN   ☐ OUT

8. Give me neither poverty nor riches, but give me only my daily bread.

   ☐ IN   ☐ OUT

9. Laughter is brightest, in the place where the food is.

   ☐ IN   ☐ OUT

10. The rich worry over their money, the poor over their bread.

    ☐ IN   ☐ OUT

197

Animals in the Bible

Which of the following phrases are in the Bible?

Check the "in" box if you think the phrase is in the Bible. Check the "out" box if you don't think it's in the Bible.

1. Whom are you pursuing? A dead dog? A flea?

   ☐ IN   ☐ OUT

2. Do horses run on the rocky crags?

   ☐ IN   ☐ OUT

3. The reason a dog has so many friends is that he wags his tail instead of his tongue.

   ☐ IN   ☐ OUT

4. A bird does not sing because it has an answer. It sings because it has a song.

   ☐ IN   ☐ OUT

5. As the deer pants for streams of water, so my soul pants for you, O God.

   ☐ IN   ☐ OUT

6. Even a live dog is better off than a dead lion!

   ☐ IN   ☐ OUT

7. Go to the ant, you sluggard; consider its ways and be wise!

   ☐ IN   ☐ OUT

8. Does a wild donkey bray when it has grass, or an ox bellow when it has fodder?

   ☐ IN   ☐ OUT

9. Like a roaring lion or a charging bear is a wicked man ruling over a helpless people.

   ☐ IN   ☐ OUT

10. A dog is man's best friend.

   ☐ IN   ☐ OUT

Living the Life

Which of the following phrases are in the Bible?

Check the "in" box if you think the phrase is in the Bible. Check the "out" box if you don't think it's in the Bible.

1. He laughs at the commotion in the town; he does not hear a driver's shout.

   ☐ **IN**   ☐ **OUT**

2. Eat to live, not live to eat.

   ☐ **IN**   ☐ **OUT**

3. A righteous man cares for the needs of his animal.

   ☐ **IN**   ☐ **OUT**

4. Early to bed, early to rise, makes a man healthy, wealthy and wise.

   ☐ **IN**   ☐ **OUT**

5. A gossip betrays a confidence, but a trustworthy man keeps a secret.

   ☐ **IN**   ☐ **OUT**

6. Children are a gift from God; they are his reward.

   ☐ **IN**   ☐ **OUT**

7. For the love of money is a root of all kinds of evil.

   ☐ **IN**   ☐ **OUT**

8. A happy heart makes the face cheerful.

   ☐ **IN**   ☐ **OUT**

9. Lazy hands make a man poor, but diligent hands bring wealth.

   ☐ **IN**   ☐ **OUT**

10. God helps them who help themselves.

    ☐ **IN**   ☐ **OUT**

Thinking About the Bible
Thinking About the People

Goal: For children to think about the people talked about in the Bible and imagine what it was like to be in their shoes.

What Do I Need?

- Bible

How Do I Do It?

- Have the children sit around you on the floor and informally discuss what it was like to be a specific Bible character. If children are unfamiliar with the Bible events, briefly tell the story (see Scripture references after each question).
- Here are some questions to get you started:
  - What do you think it was like to be inside the ark and listening to the rain on the roof? (Genesis 6—9:17)
  - What do you think it was like to be a child of one of the men who was building the Tower of Babel and suddenly hearing everyone talk in a different language? (Genesis 11:1-9)
  - What do you think it was like to be one of Joseph's brothers when the brothers sold Joseph to the traders? (Genesis 37:1-28)
  - What do you think it was like to cross the Red Sea? (Exodus 14)
  - What do you think it was like to eat manna every day? (Exodus 16:1-18)
  - What do you think it was like to see the dads and moms worship the golden calf? (Exodus 32)
  - What do you think it was like to worship in the Tabernacle? (Exodus 40:17-38)
  - What do you think it was like to live in Jericho and know that Joshua's army was walking around the walls? (Joshua 6:1-20)
  - What do you think it was like to meet Goliath while walking down the road? (1 Samuel 17:1-50)
  - What do you think it was like to be a queen visiting King Solomon's rich kingdom? (1 Kings 10:1-13)
  - What do you think it was like to see Daniel come out of the lions' den? (Daniel 6)
  - What do you think it was like to be inside a huge fish? (Jonah 1—3)
  - What do you think it was like to be a shepherd on the night Christ was born? (Luke 2:1-20)
  - What do you think it was like to be the small boy who gave Jesus the loaves and fishes? (John 6:1-13)
  - What do you think it was like to have Jesus choose you as one of His disciples? (John 1:43-49)
  - What do you think it was like to be with Paul when he went to Damascus? (Acts 9:1-19)
  - What do you think it was like to be on a missionary journey to Lystra with Paul? (Acts 14:8-20)
  - What do you think it was like to be with Paul and Silas in jail? (Acts 16:16-40)

- What do you think it was like to be Philemon and have your slave return? (Philemon)
- What do you think it was like to be John on the Isle of Patmos and write God's Word in the book of Revelation? (Revelation 1)

Take It Another Step

Give the children paper, crayons or markers and ask them to draw pictures of events from the perspective of the Bible characters.

Unscrambling the Verses

Goal: To have fun and become familiar with Bible verses at the same time.

What Do I Need?

- Bibles *(New International Version)*
- A copy of Verse Puzzles 1, 2, 3, 4, 5 or 6 (pp. 203-208) for each child
- Pencil for each child
- Small prizes

How Do I Do It?

- Give each child a pencil and a copy of the puzzle.
- Challenge the children to put the words of the verses in the right order. Children may check their answers by looking in their Bibles.
- Read the verses with the children. Ask questions such as, "What does this verse help you learn about God or Jesus? What does this verse help you learn about ways to show love and obedience to God?"
- Give prizes for those who correctly unscramble the verses.

Option

Divide the class into teams and have children on each team work together to put the words in the correct order.

Take It Another Step

Children create puzzles for each other.

Unscrambling the Verses
Verse Puzzle #1

- Unscramble the words in the following verses and write them in the correct order.
- Even if you don't know the verse, you may be able to figure out the order of the words.
- Don't look in the Bible unless your teacher tells you it's OK to do so!

1. Genesis 1:1—earth the the the beginning in God heavens and created

2. Exodus 20:12—land live Lord you honor your may mother, so that your long in the the your God is father you and giving

3. Psalms 23:1—I is my in the shepherd, shall not want Lord be

4. Psalms 100:1—joy all earth shout the for to Lord, the

5. John 3:16—that so world for his him Son God eternal only not loved in life the whoever that he gave one, believes shall and perish but have

Unscrambling the Verses
Verse Puzzle #2

- Unscramble the words in the following verses and write them in the correct order.
- Even if you don't know the verse, you may be able to figure out the order of the words.
- Don't look in the Bible unless your teacher tells you it's OK to do so!

1. John 14:1—God not let hearts me be trust in also troubled do trust in your

2. John 15:10—you commands if obey you remain love my will my in

3. Romans 3:23—God for short sinned all fall glory have of and of the

4. Philippians 4:13—strength I do through can me gives everything him who

5. 1 John 4:8—does whoever not does know love not God God love because is

Unscrambling the Verses
Verse Puzzle #3

- Unscramble the words in the following verses and write them in the correct order.
- Even if you don't know the verse, you may be able to figure out the order of the words.
- Don't look in the Bible unless your teacher tells you it's OK to do so!

1. Exodus 20:3—before you gods shall me no have other

2. Proverbs 20:11—right child even and known by a actions is his pure whether conduct by his is

3. Psalms 119:105—my and your is a to feet lamp path a my light word for

4. Matthew 19:24—easier camel eye man than go again I to is tell you kingdom a a a needle God through of it for to the of for rich enter the

5. Luke 19:10—the of to for Man came Son save seek and to what lost was

205

Unscrambling the Verses
Verse Puzzle #4

- Unscramble the words in the following verses and write them in the correct order.
- Even if you don't know the verse, you may be able to figure out the order of the words.
- Don't look in the Bible unless your teacher tells you it's OK to do so!

1. John 14:6—Father one Jesus through except answered I life way am comes to and the the the truth and no the me

2. Acts 16:31—you in household believe be the Jesus you and will and your Lord saved

3. Ephesians 6:1—parents obey is children your in this the Lord right for

4. Colossians 3:2—minds earthly set on not things things your on above

5. Philippians 4:4—say always rejoice in rejoice the again Lord I will it

Unscrambling the Verses
Verse Puzzle #5

- Unscramble the words in the following verses and write them in the correct order.
- Even if you don't know the verse, you may be able to figure out the order of the words.
- Don't look in the Bible unless your teacher tells you it's OK to do so!

1. Genesis 1:3—was light light there God let be and said and there

2. Proverbs 3:5—in the Lord understanding with your and all not on lean heart your own trust

3. Psalms 23:2—waters makes pastures quiet lie in green he he leads me me beside down

4. Proverbs 17:17—born adversity a loves at times friend and for a brother all is

5. Ecclesiastes 4:9—one two better are than return a because they good have work for their

207

Unscrambling the Verses
Verse Puzzle #6

- Unscramble the words in the following verses and write them in the correct order.
- Even if you don't know the verse, you may be able to figure out the order of the words.
- Don't look in the Bible unless your teacher tells you it's OK to do so!

1. Mark 16:15—all he to them go into creation all the world and preach the good news to said

2. John 15:13—love one friends has no greater down than he lay this that his his life for

3. Ephesians 4:32—kind be to compassionate another and other forgiving each one

4. Ephesians 6:10—strong finally Lord be in mighty the power and in his

5. 1 Thessalonians 5:22—every evil avoid kind of

Writing a Letter

Letter to a Missionary

Goal: To give children an opportunity to write to a missionary. Many children (and adults) would like to write letters to missionaries, but don't know what to say.

What Do I Need?

- Information about missionaries your church or denomination supports
- Pencils and markers or crayons
- A copy of the letter (p. 210) for each child
- Large mailing envelope and postage

How Do I Do It?

- Talk about the missionaries your church or denomination supports. Give answers to questions such as: Where do the missionaries live? What kind of work do they do? When was the last time they visited your church?
- Pray for the missionary.
- Pass out a copy of the letter to each child.
- Allow children to use crayons or markers to decorate the frame of the letter.
- Give children time to write letters or draw pictures of activities they like. Be available to help those who are having difficulty expressing themselves.

Encourage children to write about:

- School
- Their favorite free-time activities
- Their favorite foods
- What's new in your town or city (especially if the missionaries are actually from your church and know the area)
- Their favorite Bible verses and why they like them
- What they would like to know about the missionary's country (but don't promise answers from the missionaries).

You'll need to decide whether or not you want children to write both their first and last names on the letters, depending on your church's child protection policy.

- Collect letters and place in envelope. Address and add appropriate postage.

Take It Another Step

Children draw pictures for the missionary on the back of the letters.

Date _____

Dear _____,

My name is _____

I am praying for you.

Writing a Letter
Thank-You Card

Goal: To give children an opportunity to thank someone who serves at your church (pastor, musician, teacher or the person who takes care of the church yard).

What Do I Need?

- Names of people who serve at your church
- A copy of one of the cards (pp. 212-213) and envelope for each child
- Pencils, markers and/or crayons
- Whiteboard and marker or chalkboard and chalk

How Do I Do It?

- Talk about the different people who serve at your church. A good way to do this is by listing all the people needed to get one classroom ready for one class.

  Children's ministry team must find a teacher.
  Church secretary must order supplies.
  Maintenance person must clean the room.
  Teacher must study the lesson.
  Musicians must practice the music.
  Church members must give offerings to pay for the electricity, water, supplies, furniture, etc.
- Distribute cards. Children fold cards in half two times. Give children time to design and illustrate cards and write messages.

To give the children ideas of what to write in their cards, print several messages on a whiteboard or chalkboard for the children to copy or to give the children ideas what to say.

Thank you for teaching us about God.
Thank you for doing such a great job at _____
Happy Spring (or whatever season or holiday is near.)
Because of you, I am learning about Jesus.
My favorite Bible verse is _____ because
_____

You'll need to decide whether or not you want children to write both their first and last names on the letters, depending on your church's child protection policy.

Take It Another Step

Discuss how the children can help the people to whom they are writing. Children can pray for the people, pick up trash, clean up supplies, etc. Or, arrange for children to deliver cards to staff members.

211

Thank you !

Writing a Letter
Card to a Shut-in

Goal: To give children an opportunity to cheer up and encourage a shut-in.

What Do I Need?

- Information about shut-ins in your church. (Note: Make cards for the same shut-in who is having a special birthday or anniversary. Or, you could do general cards and give them to the person at your church who regularly visits the shut-ins. He or she could distribute the cards.)
- Pencils, markers and/or crayons
- A copy of one of the cards (pp. 215-216) and envelope for each child
- Whiteboard and marker or chalkboard and chalk

How Do I Do It?

- Talk about the term "shut-in." Discuss that shut-ins often aren't physically strong enough to go to church or a restaurant or to walk in the park. Sometimes shut-ins live with family, but other times, they live alone and are very lonely. Children often have a sense of compassion that surpasses even that of many adults. You will find several children doing their cards with great care.
- Pray for the shut-ins.
- Give each child a card. Children fold cards in half two times. Tell children to color the cards and then write inside messages.

You'll need to decide whether or not you want children to write both their first and last names on the letters, depending on your church's child protection policy.

You may want to look over the cards before passing them on. Sometimes children's messages are well-meaning, but not exactly comforting. Messages such as "I heard you were dying" aren't appropriate and you'll need to censor those types of cards. Write several messages on a whiteboard or chalkboard for the children to copy or to give the children ideas what to say:

> I am thinking about you today.
> Happy Spring (or whatever season or holiday is near.)
> Sending a card full of cheer your way.
> The Lord is our shepherd.
> Have a sunshiny day.

Take It Another Step

Children could do extra cards for the visitation pastor to have on hand to give to people who need a cheery "hello."

214

Writing a Letter

E-mailing a Missionary or Church Staff Member

Goal: To give children an opportunity to communicate with a missionary or church staff member.

What Do I Need?

- Large sheet of paper
- Marker
- E-mail addresses of missionaries and church staff members

How Do I Do It?

- Talk with children about the missionaries or church staff members to whom they will be sending e-mails. Explain where the missionary lives and what they do, what the church staff member's job is, etc.
- Begin the greetings as shown in the samples below. Invite children to dictate sentences for an e-mail greeting to each of the missionaries or church staff members. Print the greeting on large sheet of paper.

Dear Scott and Elizabeth,

I am sitting here with my class of fourth graders at the Main Street Church in Anywhere. We have been learning about Brazil and have been praying for you.

Here are some greetings from the kids . . .

Dear Tom,

Our class of fourth graders would like to thank you and your sons for waxing our floor last week. We all noticed how shiny it was when we came into class this morning . . .

- Take home the completed greetings and e-mail from your computer.

Take It Another Step

Pray for the missionaries and for your church.

217

Alphabet Psalm

Goal: For children to focus on praising God

What Do I Need?

- Bibles
- Copy of the Praise Psalm page (p. 219) for each group
- Markers

How Do I Do It?

- Explain the meaning of the word "psalm." "Psalm" means praise music that is usually sung or played with the harp or other instrument. Talk about some of the songs you might know that are directly from the book of Psalms.
- Divide the children into small groups.
- Challenge the children to write a psalm to God starting with each letter of the alphabet. For instance, the psalm could be something like:
  - A–Awesome
  - B–Beautiful
  - C–Creator of the Universe
  - D–Daily listens to my prayers
  - E–Everlasting

  If time is limited, children write a psalm starting with each letter of a word such as "love," "worship" or "praise."
- Children color the decorative border with markers.
- Display the completed psalms in your classroom.
- If you have an older class with several creative children, challenge them to end each couplet of the psalm with words that rhyme:
  - Awesome God up above,
  - Beautiful Savior who gives us love.

Take It Another Step

Combine several psalms from each group on a sheet of poster board and display it in a prominent place. (Make sure you use an equal number of ideas from each group.)

218

Praise Psalm

Writing a Psalm
Thanksgiving Psalm

Goal: For children to focus on praising God.

What Do I Need?

- Bibles
- Copy of the Thanksgiving Psalm page (p. 221) for each group
- Markers

How Do I Do It?

- Explain the meaning of the word "psalm." "Psalm" means praise music that is usually sung or played with the harp or other instrument. Talk about some of the songs you might know that are directly from the book of Psalms.
- Divide the children into small groups.
- Challenge the children to write something they're thankful for starting with each letter of the alphabet. For instance, the psalm could be something like:

    A–Animals
    B–Butterflies
    C–Christ
    D–Dads
    E–Everlasting life

    If time is limited, children write psalms that start with each letter of a word such as "thankful" or "thanksgiving."
- Children color the decorative border with markers.
- Display the completed psalms in your classroom.
- If you have several creative children, challenge them to end each couplet of the psalm with words that rhyme:

    I'm thankful for the animals I visit at the zoo.
    And I thank God for butterflies, yellow, green and blue.

Take It Another Step

Combine several psalms from each group on a sheet of poster board and display it in a prominent place. (Make sure you use an equal number of ideas from each group.)

Thanksgiving Psalm

221

More Great Resources from Gospel Light

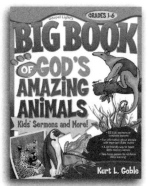

The Big Book of God's Amazing Animals
This book includes 52 lessons about a variety of animals that will intrigue kids, such as dolphins, penguins, koala bears, whales and condors. Each lesson relates facts about the featured animal to a particular Bible verse. As kids learn about fascinating animals that God created, they'll also learn about Him and how He wants them to live.
ISBN 08307.37146

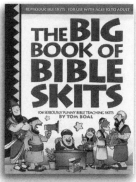

The Big Book of Bible Skits
Tom Boal

104 seriously funny Bible-teaching skits. Each skit comes with Bible background, performance tips, prop suggestions, discussion questions and more. Ages 10 to adult. Reproducible.
ISBN 08307.19164

The Really Big Book of Kids' Sermons and Object Talks with CD-ROM
This reproducible resource for children's pastors is packed with 156 sermons (one a week for three years) that are organized by topics such as friendship, prayer, salvation and more. Each sermon includes an object talk using a household object, discussion questions, prayer and optional information for older children. Reproducible.
ISBN 08307.36573

The Big Book of Volunteer Appreciation Ideas
Joyce Tepfer

This reproducible book is packed with 100 great thank-you ideas for teachers, volunteers and helpers in any children's ministry program. An invaluable resource for showing your gratitude!
ISBN 08307.33094

The Big Book of Christian Growth
Discipling made easy! 306 discussion cards based on Bible passages, and 75 games and activities for preteens. Reproducible.
ISBN 08307.25865

The Big Book of Bible Skills
Active games that teach a variety of Bible skills (book order, major divisions of the Bible, location references, key themes). Ages 8 to 12. Reproducible.
ISBN 08307.23463

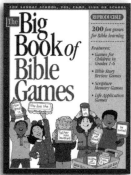

The Big Book of Bible Games
200 fun, active games to review Bible stories and verses and to apply Bible truths to everyday life. For ages 6 to 12. Reproducible.
ISBN 08307.18214

The Big Book of Bible Games #2
150 active games—balloon games, creative team relays, human bowling, and more—that combine physical activity with Bible learning. Games are arranged by Bible theme and include discussion questions. For grades 1 to 6. Reproducible.
ISBN 08307.30532

To order, visit your local Christian bookstore or www.gospellight.com

Gospel Light
God's Word for a Kid's World!™